LONGMAN

Dictionary of American English

WORKBOOK

Longman
www.longman.com

Before You Use Your Dictionary

LONGMAN Dictionary of American English

■ A A class of students was asked what features they would like to see in a dictionary. Here are their comments. Read each one and decide if you agree with them.

> The words that I am looking for should be **easy to find**. I don't want to spend a long time looking for words in a dictionary.

> A good dictionary should give me **extra information** about words. For example, it should tell me if a word is an adjective or a noun, if it is countable or uncountable, if it is a formal or informal word, and so on.

> A dictionary should tell me what a word or expression **means**, clearly and in simple language, especially if a word has more than one meaning.

> I think that a dictionary has to give students **examples** of words and expressions in sentences, so that they can see how they are used, and which words they work with.

> I have problems with spelling a lot of words. A good dictionary should be able to help me improve my **spelling**.

> A dictionary should show me how a word is **pronounced**, so that I can say it correctly.

> A dictionary should help me correct and improve my **grammar** as well as my vocabulary.

> I find all the different **word forms** for English words (for example, happy, unhappy, happiness) very complicated. These should be easy to find in a good dictionary, so that I can check I am using them correctly.

> A good dictionary shouldn't just help me to understand what a word means; it should also help me to develop my **vocabulary**, by showing me other words that are related.

> I think that a good dictionary should help me to learn "real" everyday English, such as **idioms** and **phrasal verbs**.

> It would be really helpful if the dictionary showed me useful **spoken expressions**, or expressions that I can use in different situations.

■ **B** Which features do you think you will find in your *Longman Dictionary of American English*?

Here's the good news! Your dictionary does *all* of these things. In fact, after your teacher, your *Longman Dictionary of American English* is probably the most useful and most important learning resource you will need! You will find that it helps you to develop your English in a lot of different ways.

■ **C** Now look at the Table of Contents on the next page.

Table of Contents

		Page
Title Page		1
Before You Use Your Dictionary		2
Table of Contents		4

Orientation

1	Word Order	5
2	Using Guidewords	5
3	Labels	6
4	Key Words	7
5	Cross-Referencing	8
6	Dictionary Orientation Quiz	9

Meaning

7	Definition Quiz 1	11
8	Definition Quiz 2	12
9	Picture This	13
10	Which Meaning?	14
11	Parts of Speech	16
12	Two Meanings	17
13	Signpost Matching	18
14	Fun With Puns	20

Spelling

15	Consonants and Consonant Groups	21
16	Vowels and Vowel Groups	22
17	Plurals	23
18	More Than One Spelling	23
19	Common Spelling Mistakes	24

Pronunciation

20	Identifying Pronunciation	26
21	Syllables 1	26
22	Syllables 2	27
23	Stressed Syllables	28
24	Stress Change 1	28
25	Stress Change 2	29
26	Homophones	30
27	Phonetics 1	31
28	Phonetics 2	32

Collocations

		Page
29	Example Sentences	33
30	*Do, Make,* or *Take*	34
31	Collocations 1	35
32	Collocations 2	36

Grammar

33	Irregular Verbs	37
34	Transitive and Intransitive Verbs	38
35	Grammar in Use	39
36	Common Mistakes	40

Vocabulary and Wordbuilding

37	Compound Words	41
38	Verb Prefixes	42
39	Adjective Prefixes	43
40	Thesaurus 1	44
41	Thesaurus 2	45
42	Confusing Words	46
43	Abstract Nouns	46
44	Adjective Opposites	47
45	Topic Vocabulary	48
46	Computers and the Internet	49
47	The Environment	50
48	College	51
49	Travel	52
50	Jobs	53

Phrasal Verbs

51	Phrasal Verb Chain	54
52	Hidden Phrasal Verbs	55
53	Phrasal Verb Combinations	56

Idioms

54	True or False Idioms	57
55	Body Part Idioms	58
56	Idiom Groups	59

Communication

57	Spoken Phrases	60
58	Spoken Expressions	61
	Answers	62

Orientation

1 Word Order

Your *Longman Dictionary of American English* shows words and expressions in alphabetical (A, B, C, D, etc.) order.

> **a·bate** /əˈbeɪt/ v. [I] *formal* to become less strong [➨ unabated]: *Public anger does not appear to be abating.*
> **ab·bey** /ˈæbi/ n. [C] a large church, with buildings next to it where MONKS and NUNS live
> **ab·bre·vi·ate** /əˈbriviˌeɪt/ v. [T] *formal* to make a word, story, etc. shorter: *"Street" is often* **abbreviated** *as "St.".*
> **ab·bre·vi·a·tion** /əˌbriviˈeɪʃən/ n. [C] the short form of a word used in writing. For example, Mr. is the abbreviation of Mister

> **ABC** n. **1 ABC's** [plural] the letters of the English alphabet as taught to children **2** [U] **American Broadcasting Company** one of the national companies that broadcasts television and radio programs in the U.S.
> **ab·di·cate** /ˈæbdɪˌkeɪt/ v. [I,T] **1** to officially give up the position of being king or queen **2 abdicate (your) responsibility** *formal* to refuse to continue being responsible for something —**abdication** /ˌæbdɪˈkeɪʃən/ n. [C,U]

■ Look at these words and expressions, and decide in which order they come in your dictionary. Number each one 1–17. Then check your answers in your dictionary.

☐ play-by-play	☐ palatial	☐ polyester	☐ psychology
☐ painting	☐ psalm	☐ perishable	☐ phrase
☐ phonetic	☐ poised	☐ pollution	☐ 1 painter
☐ Ph.D.	☐ poisonous	☐ plaster of Paris	☐ perish
☐ palace			

2 Using Guidewords

You will find a guideword in the top corner of each page. These guidewords tell you what the first and last words on the pages are. Knowing this will help you to find words more quickly.

> **abide**
> **a·bide** /əˈbaɪd/ v. [T] **can't abide sb/sth** to hate someone or something very much: *I can't abide his stupid jokes.*

> **absolve**
> **abs** /æbz/ n. [plural] *informal* the muscles on your ABDOMEN (=stomach): *exercises that strengthen your abs*

■ Here are the guidewords for pages 40 and 41 of your dictionary. Circle the words and expressions in the box that you think can be found on these pages.

> **aquatic**
> ZODIAC, represented by a person pouring water **2** [C] someone born between January 20 and February 18

> **armed**
> **a·ri·a** /ˈɑriə/ n. [C] a song that is sung by only one person in an OPERA

| area code | around | armchair | armful | arable |
| arithmetic | approximate | aquarium | arduous | Arctic |

3 Labels

Your dictionary gives you lots of extra information about the words and expressions you will find and use. It uses *labels* to give you this information.

they /ðeɪ/ *pron.* **1** the people or things that have already been mentioned or that are already known about: *Ken gave me these flowers – aren't they beautiful?* | *I stopped at Doris and Ed's place, but*

pron. tells us that *they* is a pronoun.

de·duce /dɪˈdus/ *v.* [T] *formal* to make a judgment based on the information that you have

v., [T], and *formal* tell us that *deduce* is a verb, it is *transitive*, and it is used in *formal* situations.

child·ish /ˈtʃaɪldɪʃ/ *adj.* **1** *disapproving* behaving in a silly way that makes you seem younger than you really are [= **immature**]: *Stop being so childish.* **2** relating to or typical of a child: *a childish game* —**childishly** *adv.*

adj., *disapproving* + [= **immature**] tell us that *childish* is an *adjective*, we use it when we want to *disapprove* of something, and that *immature* has exactly the same meaning.

■ **A   Complete these sentences with a *label*. Use your dictionary to help you.**

1   ***adj.*** means that a word is an ___adjective___. *Happy* and *sad* are just two examples.

2   **[U]** means that a noun is _____. *Water*, *bread*, and *rice* are three examples.

3   Words such as *foe* have the word _____ after them. This means that they are mostly used in literature and poems, and are not usually used in essays.

4   *Walkman*, *Coke*, *Thermos*, and *Jell-O* are examples of _____ names.

5   If somebody is described as *chicken*, it means that they are easily afraid. When *chicken* is used in this way, it is an _____ word.

6   Nouns such as *outcome* are _____, and cannot have a plural form.

7   If something is very good, we say that it is <u>really</u> good. However, some people say <u>real</u> good. This is an example of _____ English, and you should not use it in essays.

8   Some words, like *childlike*, are used in an _____ way. If a person uses this word to describe somebody, they approve of them (if they disapprove, they would use the word *childish*).

9   ***sb*** is an abbreviation for *somebody*, ***sth*** is an abbreviation for _____.

10 *Larynx* is an example of a _____ word. Words like this relate to particular subjects such as science, medicine, etc.

11 ***phr. v.*** is an abbreviation for _____. *Take off*, *give away*, and *make out* are typical examples.

12 ***prep.*** is an abbreviation for _____. *In*, *at*, *on*, and *under* are just four examples.

6   Orientation

■ **B** Copy the answers from Activity A in the blanks below. Discover the secret word in the shaded column.

	A	D	J	E	C	T	I	V	E	
1										
2										
3										
4										
5										
6										
7										
8										
9										
10										
11										
12										

4 Key Words

Some words in the *Longman Dictionary of American English* are printed in red. These are *key words*. This means that they are the words we use the most often in our written and spoken English.

■ **A** Look at page 3 in your dictionary. How many *key words* can you find? _____

■ **B** Look at these groups of words. In each group, there is <u>one</u> *key word*. Which word do you think is the *key word* in each case? Circle it. Check your answers in your dictionary.

1	aloud	alternate	always	alphabet	alright
2	kettle	keep	ketchup	keen	keel
3	receiver	recycle	rectangle	reflect	record
4	new	neutral	nest	negotiate	necessity
5	worksheet	word	worm	workman	wobble
6	exposure	expressway	extinct	expression	extreme
7	theft	thaw	thanks	thief	that
8	yogurt	yoga	you	yawn	yacht
9	leap	learn	leak	least	legend

5 Cross-Referencing

> **bet¹** /bɛt/ *v.* past tense and past participle **bet**, present participle **betting** **1** [I, T] to risk money on the result of a race, game, competition, or other future event (→ **gamble**). *She bet all her money on a horse that came in last.* | *I bet him $20 that he wouldn't do it.*

Arrows like these → refer you to other related words and expressions in the dictionary. These include words which have a similar meaning, an opposite meaning, or words which might be used in the same context.

> *break/crack the enemy's code.* **3** [C] a set of numbers, letters, or symbols that give you information about something: *Goods that you order must have a product code.* → AREA CODE, BAR CODE, ZIP CODE

Arrows like these → refer you to compound words that are made up of the word you are looking for, and another word.

A Look up the words in **bold** in your dictionary. Use the arrows to find the answers to these questions.

1 If **homework** is work for school that a student does at home, what is the word for the work you do in the house (for example, cleaning and washing clothes)? _housework_

2 Replace the word in bold with one which is more appropriate:

"He had to climb onto the **ceiling** to repair the TV antenna." _____

3 What is the noun of the verb **choose**? _____

4 Unscramble the letters in italics to make a word:

A *plopat* is a small **computer**. _____

5 What is the word for a male **cow**? _____

6 You put your **cup** on one of these when you drink tea or coffee. _____

7 What is the noun of the adjective **deep**? _____

8 A **hero** is the main male character in a book or film, but what is the main *female* character? _____

9 Complete this sentence:

A _____ is a small **horse**.

10 Complete this sentence:

We use **pots** and _____ to put food in when we cook it, and we use a _____ to hold and pour liquids like water and milk.

11 An **outpatient** is somebody who goes to hospital for treatment but does not stay there. What do we call somebody who goes to hospital for treatment and stays there? _____

12 A mountain can be described as **high**. Can we use this word to describe a tree? _____

8 Orientation

B Write compound words using the words in the box. Then look up the words in the box in your dictionary to see if you were correct.

affair	aid	angle	animal	being	belt
bird	board	disk	~~father~~	finger	food

step _father_   human _____   right _____

health _____   floppy _____   black _____

early _____   index _____   financial _____

seat _____   love _____   party _____

6 Dictionary Orientation Quiz

Use your dictionary to find the answers to these questions. Circle or write in the correct answers.

Look at page 1 of your dictionary:

1. Where will you find information about the difference between *a* and *an*?
   a) in the main entry
   b) in a Thesaurus box
   c) in a Grammar box
   d) in a Topic box

2. In the entry for *abduct*, you will see this: *(= kidnap)*. What does this mean?
   a) *Kidnap* is the opposite of *abduct*.
   b) *Kidnap* has the same meaning as *abduct*.

3. Where would you look in your dictionary to find the meaning of *abet*? Is this word usually used on its own, or must it be used with other words? _____

Look at page 2 of your dictionary:

4. The word *abide* is followed by the words *can't abide*. Why do you think these words are here?
   _____

5. What is the plural of *ability*?
   a) abilitys   b) abiliteis   c) abilities   d) abilityes   e) there is no plural form

6. In the entry for *abnormal*, you will see this: *(≠ normal)*. What does this mean?
   a) *Normal* has the same meaning as *abnormal*.
   b) *Normal* has the opposite meaning of *abnormal*.
   c) The word *normal* does not exist.

7. What other word has the same meaning as *about*[2]? _____

Orientation   9

Look at page 3 of your dictionary:

8 Where can you find the adverb *abruptly*?
   a) at the beginning of the entry *abrupt*
   b) at the end of the entry *abrupt*
   c) as a separate entry

9 Where can you find the adverb *absolutely*?
   a) at the beginning of the entry *absolute*
   b) at the end of the entry *absolute*
   c) as a separate entry

10 a) What four words have the same, or a similar, meaning as *absolutely*?

   b) Where would you look in your dictionary to find these four words together?

Look at page 4 of your dictionary:

11 If you don't understand the meaning of the second sense of the word *abstract*[1], where else could you look in your dictionary?

12 If you wanted more information about how the word *accelerate* is used, where would you look in your dictionary?

Look at page 5 of your dictionary:

13 A friend asks you out for a meal, and you want to accept. What could you say to your friend?

Look at page 6 of your dictionary:

14 What other word can be used instead of *acclimate*, with exactly the same meaning?

Look at page 10 of your dictionary:

15 Find two *informal* expressions which use the noun *act*.

16 Are the nouns *act* and *action* used in exactly the same way?

Look at page 14 of your dictionary:

17 In the entry for *adulthood*, you will see this: ➡ **childhood**. What does this mean?
   a) *childhood* has the same meaning as *adulthood*
   b) *childhood* is related to *adulthood* in some way
   c) *childhood* is the opposite of *adulthood*

Meaning

7 Definition Quiz 1

For many students, finding out the meaning, or *definition*, of a word is the most important reason for using a dictionary. Your *Longman Dictionary of American English* gives clear, easy-to-understand definitions of words you will come across.

> **can·yon** /ˈkænyən/ *n.* [C] a deep valley with very steep sides: *the Grand Canyon*

■ **Do this general knowledge quiz. Check your answers in your dictionary.**

1 What kind of person would use a *pseudonym*?

2 At what time of the year is *Lent*?

3 Which of these adjectives best describes *curry*? Circle the correct answer.

   a) bland   b) hot   c) sweet   d) bitter   e) sour

4 Who would you go see if you had problems with one of your *molars*?

5 True or false: *senile* people are very young.

6 What would you carry in a *Thermos*? Circle the correct answer.

   a) a drink   b) an animal   c) your dinner   d) a baby   e) pens and pencils

7 Which animal does *venison* come from?

8 What are *cocoons* made out of?

9 What kind of person sits on a *throne*?

10 What would you keep in an *IRA*?

11 Where would you find a *snout*? Circle the correct answer.

   a) on a teapot   b) in a police station   c) on a car   d) on a pig   e) by a river

12 What kind of animal is an *anchovy*?

8 Definition Quiz 2

■ **Practice using your dictionary to find out what a word means.**

1. A *greenback* is an informal word for a _____.
   a) farmer   b) dollar bill   c) fast-food restaurant   d) Congressman

2. How much money is a) a *dime* _____ b) a *quarter* _____ and c) a *nickel* _____?

3. Complete this sentence with one word: An academic year is divided into two *semesters* or four _____.

4. The U.S. flag is known as the *Stars and* _____.
   a) *Spots*   b) *Stripes*   c) *Lines*   d) *Checks*

5. True or false: the name of the U.S. national anthem is *The Star-Spangled Flag*.

6. Which of the following is *not* a public holiday?
   a) Labor Day   b) Independence Day   c) Memorial Day   d) President's Day   e) Thanksgiving
   f) Martin Luther King Day   g) Groundhog Day

7. Which of these two groups of elected people is the largest, the *Senate* or the *House of Representatives*? _____

8. What does the *D.C.* stand for in *Washington, D.C.*? _____

9. What is the name of the building in Washington, D.C. where Congress meets and makes laws?
   a) the White House   b) the Capitol   c) the Pentagon   d) the Oval Office

10. Complete this sentence: A *grade school* is also known as a(n) _____ school.

11. In which part of the U.S.A. would you find the *Ivy League* colleges?
    a) the south-west   b) the south-east   c) the north-west   d) the north-east

12. What would you do at a *drive-in*? _____

13. What would you do at a *prom*? _____

14. What do people mean when they talk about the *American Dream*? _____
_____

9 Picture This

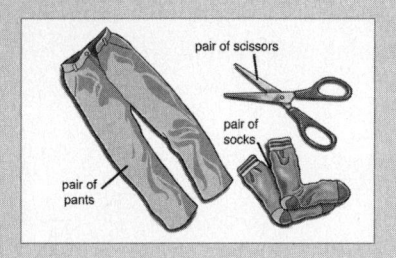

Your dictionary contains pictures that will help you understand a word more clearly. Some pictures are grouped under a particular topic, such as transportation, vegetables, etc. This picture is taken from the entry *pair*.

■ **Read the definitions to complete the crossword. To help you, find the picture at each word in bold.**

Across
3   A large, shiny, dark purple fruit that is cooked and eaten as a vegetable (**vegetable**).
5   The short, thick finger on the side of your hand, that helps you to hold things (**hand**).
7   A piece of material that you wear around your neck, head, or shoulders to keep you warm or make you look attractive (**clothes**).
9   A painting, drawing, or photograph of a person (**painting**).
10   One of the small hairs that grow on the edge of your eyelid (**eye**).
11   To move by making short, quick jumps (**jump**).
12   A long seat for two or more people, especially outside (**seat**).
13   To rub food such as cheese, vegetables, etc. against a rough or sharp surface, in order to break it into small pieces (**cut**).

Down
1   A light, soft shoe that you wear in your house (**shoe**).
2   A heavy cover that keeps you warm in bed (**bed**).
4   Hair that grows on a man's upper lip (**hair**).
6   A band or chain that you wear around your wrist or arm as decoration (**jewelry**).
7   A small, hard object produced by plants, from which a new plant will grow (**fruit**).
8   A small electric light that you carry in your hand (**light**).
12   A type of bread that is shaped like a ring (**bread**).

Meaning   13

10 Which Meaning?

Many English words have more than one meaning. If a word in your dictionary has more than one meaning, you will see a number (1, 2, 3, etc.) before each meaning or *definition*.

> **ice¹** /aɪs/ *n.* ①[U] water that has frozen into a solid: *Do you want some ice in your drink?* | *There's too much ice and snow on the roads.* ② **break the ice** to begin to be friendly to someone by talking to him/her: *Stan tried to break the ice by asking her where she was from.*

ice (noun) has two meanings, so each one is numbered.
The first meaning is the most common one, but you shouldn't forget to look at the other meanings as well.

■ **Look at the pairs of pictures below. Look up the word in bold in the dictionary, and write the number of the meaning that matches each picture.**

1   **bow**   2   _____

2   **buck**   _____   _____

3   **star**   _____   _____

14   Meaning

4   **bar**

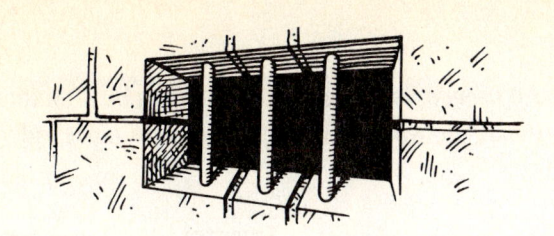

5   **pin**

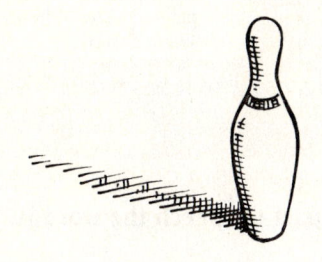

6   **suit**

7   **chicken**

8   **frame**

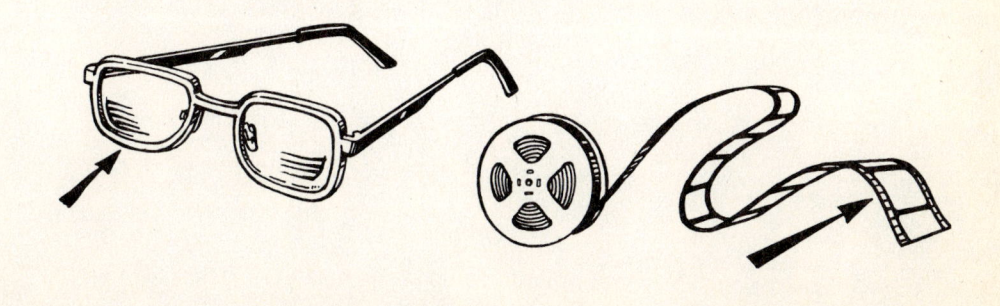

Meaning   15

11 Parts of Speech

Many words can be different parts of speech. For example, a word can be a noun as well as a verb or an adjective. In cases like these, the word will appear as two or more individual entries in your dictionary.

fa·vor·ite¹ /ˈfeɪvrɪt, -vərɪt/ *adj.* your favorite person or thing is the one you like most: *Who's your favorite actor?* | *My favorite sport is baseball.* ▶ Don't say "most favorite." ◀

favorite² *n.* [C] **1** something that you like more than others of the same kind: *I like all her books, but this one is my favorite.* **2** someone who is liked and treated better than others by a teacher or parent: *Katie was always Mom's favorite.* **3** the team, person, etc. that is expected to win a competition: *The Yankees are favorites to win the World Series.*

In this example, *favorite* can be an *adjective* and a *noun*, so it has two entries, one for each part of speech.

■ Look up the words in **bold** to find out which part of speech the word is. Write the part of speech in the sentence in the column.

	Sentence	Part of Speech
1	We're **about** to leave.	*adjective*
2	The **access** to the library is at the back of the school.	
3	You should **address** your teacher as "Mr. Harris," and not "Hey, you."	
4	I want to do something that will help me **advance** my position in this company.	
5	He thought he would fail the test, but he passed **after** all.	
6	You can't go to the bar because you're under **age**.	
7	We knew **all** along that the test would be difficult.	
8	He never **answers** any of my e-mails.	

12 Two Meanings

Each of the words in the box has two different meanings. Complete the sentences using each word in two sentences. Check your answers in your dictionary.

| climate | depressed | medicine | generous | study (verb) |

1 A substance used for treating illness: *He's always forgetting to take his _____.*

2 Not having enough jobs or business activity to make an area, industry, etc., successful: *a _____ economy.*

3 To spend time going to classes, reading, etc., to learn about a subject: *I need to _____ for a midterm.*

4 Someone who is kind, and enjoys giving people things or helping them: *She was _____ to strangers as well as to her friends.*

5 The typical weather conditions in an area: *a hot and humid _____.*

6 The treatment and study of illnesses and injuries: *Joe is studying _____ at college.*

7 Very sad: *He felt _____ about failing the test.*

8 To examine something carefully to find out more about it: *Dr. Brock is going to _____ how the disease affects children.*

9 The general feelings in a situation at a particular time: *in the current _____ of uncertainty.*

10 More than the usual amount: *a _____ slice of cake.*

Meaning

13 Signpost Matching

When words have many different meanings, your dictionary uses *signposts* to help you find the meaning you want more quickly. Each signpost is followed by a definition of the word (and usually an example sentence).

> **clear**[1] /klɪr/ *adj.*
> 1 SIMPLE/EASY easy to understand, hear, read, or see: *clear instructions | The law is quite clear on this issue. | Smith was very clear about the school's policies on the matter. | It is clear to me that the company will have to make further job cuts. | Have I made myself clear? | Hugh had made it perfectly clear (that) he wasn't interested. | We must send out a clear message/signal to voters.*
>
> **THESAURUS**
> noticeable, obvious, conspicuous, striking, eye-catching
> → see Thesaurus box at NOTICEABLE
>
> 2 CERTAIN impossible to doubt: *clear evidence | It's not clear how it happened. | It became clear that he would soon die. | a clear case/example of fraud | In this situation, there is no clear winner.*
> 3 SURE ABOUT STH [not before noun] feeling sure that you understand something [≠ **confused**]: *I'm not clear about what you want me to do.*
> 4 SEE THROUGH easy to see through: *clear glass bottles | a clear mountain lake*
> 5 WEATHER weather that is clear is bright with no rain or clouds: *a clear sky*
> 6 NOT BLOCKED not blocked, hidden, or covered by anything: *a clear view of the harbor | smooth clear skin*

In this example, *clear* has six signposts.

■ **A** On the left, you can see 9 signposts for the verb *run*. In the grid on the right, you can see 9 sample sentences.

Work in pairs. Match each signpost with the correct example sentence.

1	MOVE	Some cars *run* on diesel.	
2	BE IN CHARGE OF STH	Beth *runs* a bar in Soho.	
3	IN A RACE	Check that the software will *run* on your computer.	
4	MACHINES	We decided to *run* an ad in the *Houston Chronicle*.	8
5	COMPUTERS	Tears started to *run* down her cheeks.	
6	ELECTION	I've decided to *run* in the Boston Marathon.	
7	MONEY/NUMBERS	She turned and *ran* away.	
8	NEWS/STORIES/ADVERTISEMENTS	Inflation was *running* at 10.5%.	
9	WATER/LIQUIDS	He is *running* for a seat in the Senate.	

18 Meaning

B Now do the same with this one, matching the signposts with the different meanings of *point*.

1	ONE IDEA	The whole *point* of this new law is to protect people.	
2	MAIN IDEA	At that *point* in my life I was still single.	
3	PURPOSE	The Los Angeles Lakers are leading by four *points*.	
4	IN TIME/DEVELOPMENT	Two *point* four million dollars were spent on the project.	8
5	QUALITY	The stars shone like *points* of light in the sky.	
6	GAME/SPORT	He made several useful *points* at yesterday's meeting.	
7	SMALL SPOT	I wish you'd get to the *point*!	
8	IN NUMBERS	I waited for her at the *point* where the two paths meet.	
9	PLACE	One of his weak *points* is that he easily gets upset.	

C Match these signposts with the different meanings of *call*.

1	TELEPHONE	I decided to *call* the meeting for Friday afternoon.	
2	DESCRIBE	We had to go stand in line when he *called* our names.	
3	ASK/ORDER	She *called* him an idiot for wasting his money.	
4	ARRANGE	"Wait for me!" Bob *called*.	
5	SAY/SHOUT	What are you going to *call* the new puppy?	
6	NAME	I told him I'd *call* him sometime later today.	
7	READ NAMES	You'd better *call* the police.	

D Check your answers in your dictionary (note that the numbers in the exercise and the numbers in your dictionary do not always correspond). Who made the most correct matches?

Meaning 19

14 Fun with Puns

A *pun* is a joke that uses one word with two different meanings. Complete each pun below by writing a word from the box. You will need to change the form of some of the words. Use your dictionary to help you. Look carefully at the different meanings of the words in the box.

| beat | charge | change | bar | crack |
| call | bright | bill | horn | atmosphere |

1 Why did the teacher need to wear sunglasses?
   Because his students were so _____.

2 Alice just swallowed a handful of dimes!
   Really? I haven't noticed any _____ in her.

3 Why should you never have a party on the moon?
   Because there's no _____!

4 Policeman: I'm arresting you.
   Man: What's the _____?
   Policeman: Nothing. It's free.

5 A man walked into a _____. Ouch! It was an iron _____.

6 Why do cows wear bells?
   Because their _____ don't work.

7 The cook at our school is really mean. Yesterday I saw her _____ some eggs.

8 Could you _____ me a cab?
   Sure. You're a cab.

9 Mom, there's a duck at the door in a hat.
   Don't be silly, dear. That's a man with a _____.

10 The police arrested an egg yesterday. After six hours of interrogation, it finally _____.

20 Meaning

Spelling

LONGMAN Dictionary of American English

Many of the exercises in the Spelling section also deal with pronunciation. This is because some spellings are pronounced differently, for example en**ough** and thr**ough**.
On the other hand, different spellings can have the same pronunciation. For example, the first sound for the words **n**ew, **pn**eumonia, and **kn**ife is the same: /n/ (you do not pronounce the *p* in *pneumonia* or the *k* in *knife*).
There is a pronunciation table on the inside front cover of your dictionary.

15 Consonants and Consonant Groups

Match the words in the box with the correct sounds. The sounds to match are in **bold** in the words. You need to find 4 words for each column. Then check your answers in your dictionary.

knee	**wr**ong	**c**ream	**th**eater	re**s**ult
ma**ch**ine	**n**ever	**rh**ino	per**h**aps	**g**uest
zebra	**ps**ychology	**p**icture	**s**ugar	**j**aguar
~~ki**tch**en~~	**ph**ysical	**h**igh	**p**oetry	na**t**ure
gopher	**sh**ore	**c**oncert	**kn**ow	**w**ater
hello	**pn**eumonia	**wh**at	**j**udge	**th**ink
theory	**sc**ene	**l**augh	**j**acket	day**s**
gather	fi**n**ger	**k**ind	**th**ere	**q**uick
for**g**et	a**g**ree	**p**eace	**p**ath	for**w**ard
when	**ch**eck	**th**ough	**o**pen	**s**tation
come	e**dge**	ari**s**e	**p**ay	**h**urry
see	f**r**uit	**wh**o	**th**at	**r**ice

/tʃ/ as in wa**tch**	/k/ as in **k**ey	/f/ as in **f**antastic	/s/ as in **s**ettle	/ʃ/ as in **sh**ip
kitchen				

/n/ as in **n**ight	/r/ as in **r**ight	/z/ as in ga**z**e	/dʒ/ as in **j**ump	/p/ as in **p**en

/h/ as in **h**eavy	/w/ as in **W**ednesday	/g/ as in **g**ame	/θ/ as in **th**ing	/ð/ as in **th**e

Spelling 21

16 Vowels and Vowel Groups

A One letter or group of letters may have more than one sound. Look in your dictionary to find out how the letters *ou* are pronounced in each of these words.

thr**ou**gh   alth**ou**gh   b**ou**gh   t**ou**gh   c**ou**gh

B One sound may be shown by more than one letter or group of letters. Look at the letters in **bold** in the words below. Two of them have a different sound than the other ones. Use your dictionary to find which ones and circle them.

thr**ou**gh   p**u**ll   tr**ue**   r**ou**gh   st**u**dent   b**oo**t   thr**ew**

C Look at the letters in **bold** in the words below. Match the words that have the same sound by writing them in the correct column.

w**ei**rd thr**ow** st**y**le b**oy** **eye** f**a**sten d**o**g b**ea**r w**a**ll m**o**ther l**au**gh p**ai**d b**o**red j**aw** t**o**ne s**ai**d f**ee**d t**y**pical g**au**ge thr**ea**t s**ui**te r**oa**r f**a**ther br**ea**k b**uy** h**ei**ght w**ou**ld ph**o**tograph w**o**nderful st**ai**r d**ea**r m**o**re h**ow** w**ei**gh m**u**rder ach**ie**ve gener**a**lity t**ou**ch c**ei**ling c**au**ght c**a**mp**aig**n

/i/ as in b**ea**t	/ɪ/ as in b**i**t	/eɪ/ as in d**a**te	/æ/ as in b**a**t	/ɛ/ as in b**e**t
feed				

/ʊ/ as in b**oo**k	/ɑ/ as in b**o**x	/ʌ/ as in b**u**t	/ɔ/ as in b**ou**ght	/oʊ/ as in b**oa**t

/ə/ as in b**a**nana	/ɚ/ as in sh**i**rt	/aɪ/ as in b**i**te	/aʊ/ as in ab**ou**t	/ɔɪ/ as in v**oi**ce

/ɪr/ as in b**ee**r	/ɛr/ as in b**a**re	/ɔr/ as in d**oo**r

D Check your answers in your dictionary.

17 Plurals

Your dictionary shows you the plural forms of some nouns, especially irregular nouns that do not end with -s, or which include extra letters before the -s.

> **fish**¹ /fɪʃ/ *n.* plural **fish** or **fishes** **1** [C] an animal that lives in water and uses its FINS and tail to swim: *How many fish did you catch?* **2** [U] the flesh of a fish used as food: *We had fish for dinner.*

In this example, the plural of *fish* can be either *fish* or *fishes*.

■ **The plural words in bold are spelled incorrectly. Write the correct plural form on each line. Check your answers in your dictionary.**

1. The police found several **knifes** hidden in a box in the attic. ___knives___
2. Students are grouped according to their **abilitys** and interests. _____
3. We had a boring meal of meatloaf and **potatos**. _____
4. Bob's Music Store sells the largest selection of **pianoes** and guitars in the city. _____
5. A lot of **countrys** signed the Kyoto Agreement, but some have already changed their minds. _____
6. All of the **womans** there have complained about his behavior. _____
7. The Internet, television, and radio are all powerful advertising **mediums**. _____
8. Several **busses** depart daily for New York City. _____
9. I knew quite a few **persons** at the party. _____
10. We found a nest of **mouses** hiding behind the refrigerator. _____

18 More Than One Spelling

Your dictionary shows you if a word can be spelled in more than one way. The alternative spelling comes second if the two spellings are very similar. The first spelling is the most common one.

> **en·roll**, **enrol** /ɪnˈroʊl/ *v.* [I,T] to officially join a school, university, etc., or to arrange for someone else to do this.: *the students enrolled in honors classes* | *Nathan enrolled at City College.*

If the spellings are very different, each spelling has its own entry. The less common spelling has a cross-reference to the more common spelling.

■ **In each of these sentences, circle the spelling you think is more common. Check your answers in your dictionary.**

1. Students who wish to **enrol/enroll** in the class should arrive by 9:30.
2. The **dialogue/dialog** in the movie didn't seem very natural.
3. The food in that restaurant is a little **pricy/pricey**.
4. The sky was **gray/grey**, and it was raining hard.
5. She was surrounded by all the **glamor/glamour** of Hollywood.
6. My kids hate the taste of strawberry **jello/Jell-O**.
7. Turn the computer on before you insert the **disc/disk**.
8. I ordered the dress from a mail-order **catalog/catalogue**.

19 Common Spelling Mistakes

Look at the sentences below. The words in **bold** are spelled incorrectly. Write the correct spelling in the crossword grid. Check your answers in your dictionary.

Across
- 4 Congress needs to address the problem of **persistant** unemployment.
- 7 The **goverment** has just announced its spending plans for next year.
- 10 She managed to **acheive** her ambition of becoming a lawyer.
- 11 The whole nation **bennefited** from having skilled and educated workers.
- 13 **Cole** miners went on strike to demand higher wages.
- 15 This **stile** of furniture is very popular nowadays.
- 16 The box didn't **contane** anything except a pair of old socks.
- 17 There has been a lot of criticism directed at the **advertizing** industry.
- 18 She and her husband had had a huge **arguement**.
- 21 I'm ten pounds **overwait** and really need to go on a diet.
- 22 He was a very old man with **narled** hands and a hunched back.
- 26 Her **nowledge** of current affairs is useful in her job.
- 27 He took several **photografs** of the temple.
- 28 We decided to take a **peacefull** vacation in the mountains.
- 29 All the children have **seperate** bedrooms.

24 Spelling

Down

1. It's not easy to **gage** exactly what her response will be.
2. Keiko's English **pronounciation** has improved a lot recently.
3. A ladder leads from the third floor to the **atic**.
5. I went to extra classes because I wanted to gain **fluensy** in Spanish.
6. During Jack's **abcences**, Stephen acted as manager.
8. It is a very **effishent** company, which has performed extremely well.
9. Finding ways to reduce costs is a **chalenging** problem.
10. He **adviced** her to read the contract carefully before signing it.
12. We began a **campain** to make people more aware of the problems of poverty.
14. I'm **cannceling** tomorrow's meeting because so many people will be on vacation.
15. Isaac Newton was the founder of modern **sience**.
19. This movie is **tipical** of his work.
20. I can't wear this skirt. It's got too many **rinkles**.
23. In the sixth year of **drowt**, almost half the corn crop was lost.
24. Unfortunately, we weren't able to get in **tuch** with you earlier.
25. Nobody recognized him after he had shaved his **beird** off.

Pronunciation

LONGMAN Dictionary of American English

There are 26 letters and 47 pronunciation symbols in American English. There is a complete pronunciation table on the inside front cover of your *Longman Dictionary of American English*.

Many of the exercises in the Pronunciation section also deal with spelling. This is because some sounds are spelled in different ways. For example, the first sound in the words **n**ew, **pn**eumonia, and **kn**ife is the same: /n/.

On the other hand, the same spelling can be pronounced differently, for example eno**ugh** and thro**ugh**.

20 Identifying Pronunciation

Your dictionary shows you how every word is pronounced, by using pronunciation symbols. These symbols will help you find out quickly how to pronounce a word (unlike many languages, letters or groups of letters in English can be pronounced in more than one way).

> **En·glish¹** /ˈɪŋɡlɪʃ/ n. **1** [U] the language used in places such as the U.S., Canada, and Great Britain **2 the English** [plural] the people of England

> **bed¹** /bɛd/ n. **1** [C,U] a piece of furniture for sleeping on: *a **double bed** (=a bed for two people)* | *a **single bed** (=a bed for one person)* | *I was lying **in bed** reading.* | *She looked like she had just **gotten out of bed**.* | *What time do you usually **put** the kids **to bed**?* | *Jamie usually **goes to bed** around seven o'clock.* | *Sara, have you **made** your*

In these examples, the letter *e* is pronounced differently in the two words.

■ **A** Look at these words. The letter o is pronounced differently in each word except in two of them which are pronounced the same way. Circle these words. Check your answers in your dictionary.

t**o**mb   c**o**mb   b**o**mb   **o**nce   sh**o**ck   **o**ccur

■ **B** Look at these words. The letters in **bold** are pronounced the same way in all the words except one. Circle the word that is pronounced differently. Check your answers in your dictionary.

shut   **ch**agrin   examina**ti**on   spe**ci**al   concu**ssi**on   wa**tch**ful

21 Syllables 1

The word at the beginning of each entry in your dictionary is divided into syllables, separated by a •. Each syllable contains a single vowel sound, no matter how it is spelled. *Original* has four syllables: o + rig + i + nal

> **o·rig·i·nal¹** /əˈrɪdʒənl/ adj. **1** [only before noun] first or earliest: *Our original plan was to go to Florida.* | *The original version of the song is much better.*

Some words only have one syllable, such as *speak*.

26   Pronunciation

NOTE: *-ted* and *-ded* endings on past tense verbs, and *-ted* endings on adjectives (wil<u>ted</u>, wan<u>ted</u>, wa<u>ded</u>, etc.) are always pronounced as an individual syllable (wilt•ed, want•ed, wad•ed). Others (for example, *-ped*, *-ked*, etc.) are usually not (taped, walked, cheered, killed), but there are exceptions with some adjectives (for example, *crook•ed*, *rag•ged*).

■ **Look at each word carefully and decide how many syllables each one has. Insert a syllable point (•) *if* and *where* you think that one is needed.**

1	expropriate	8	defunct	15	warped
2	fragrance	9	seismic	16	pigeon
3	operate	10	realm	17	involvement
4	original	11	luxurious	18	advertisement
5	sympathetic	12	incinerate	19	discussion
6	indication	13	Wednesday	20	physique
7	doubt	14	retire	21	hairstyle

Check your answers in your dictionary.

22 Syllables 2

■ **Write the words in the correct column. Check your answers in your dictionary.**

<u>advertisement</u>   cracked   justifiable   representative   radio   crooked   unfortunately   hedge   fruition   enjoyable   classified   indication   compute   junior   cooked   laugh   periodical   overburdened   fruitless   sympathize

1 Syllable	2 Syllables	3 Syllables	4 Syllables	5 Syllables
			advertisement	

Pronunciation   27

23 Stressed Syllables

If a word has more than one syllable, one of the syllables is usually spoken more strongly than the others. This is called *stress*. Most words have one stressed syllable. Longer words may have a *secondary stress*, or lighter stress, on another syllable.

Stress is a very important feature of pronunciation. If you do not stress a word correctly, people may not understand what you are saying.

> **jus·tice** /ˈdʒʌstɪs/ *n.* **1** [U] fairness in the way people are treated [≠ **injustice**]: *If there were any*

> **jus·ti·fi·a·ble** /ˌdʒʌstəˈfaɪəbəl/ *adj.* an action, decision, etc. that is justifiable is reasonable

Justice is stressed on its <u>first</u> syllable. *Justifiable* is stressed on its <u>third</u> syllable, but is also has a *secondary* or lighter stress on its <u>first</u> syllable.

A Underline the syllables that are pronounced more strongly than the others. Check your answers in your dictionary.

a<u>bout</u>	seasonal	agreeable	employ	accompany	arrogant
photographer	hockey	security	pronounce	appearance	seriously
adjective	conclusion	teacher	argument		

B These words have a main stress and a secondary stress. Circle the main stress and underline the secondary stress in each one.

| <u>ac</u>a(de)mic | accommodation | aftershave | alphabet | artificial | assassination |

24 Stress Change 1

A These words can be either a verb or a noun. The stressed syllable of each verb is underlined. If the stress changes when the word is used as a noun, underline the new stressed syllable.

verb	noun	verb	noun
in<u>crease</u>	<u>in</u>crease	re<u>bel</u>	rebel
in<u>sult</u>	insult	per<u>mit</u>	permit
re<u>fund</u>	refund	de<u>sert</u>	desert
con<u>duct</u>	conduct	pro<u>duce</u>	produce
pre<u>sent</u>	present	sus<u>pect</u>	suspect
ob<u>ject</u>	object	pro<u>test</u>	protest

B Now complete these sentences with the words above. The same word should be used to complete both blanks in each sentence (once as a noun, once as a verb). Not all the words are used.

1 Nobody went to the ___protest___ because nobody had anything to ___protest___ about.
2 I asked for a _____, but the store refused to _____ me anything.
3 You need a _____ to park that will _____ you to park your car in the private garage.
4 He's kind of a _____, but I don't think he has much to _____ about.
5 We'd like to _____ you with a small _____ before you go.
6 Farmers work hard to _____ all of the _____, such as fruits and vegetables, that we buy at the supermarket.
7 He shouted an _____ at me, but I refused to _____ him back.
8 The manager wanted to _____ prices by 50%, but the _____ was opposed by her employees.
9 What a horrible _____! Where did you find it? I really _____ to you bringing it into the office.
10 After the expedition team reached the middle of the _____, their leader decided to _____ them.

C Work in pairs. Read the sentences out loud, making sure that you pronounce each word correctly. Check in your dictionary if the pronunciation of any of the vowels changes.

25 Stress Change 2

The position of the stress often changes when a new word is formed from another word. In some cases, the pronunciation of some syllables changes when the stress changes.

Look at these word pairs. The main stress in the first word is underlined. If the stress is different in the second word underline the new stressed syllable. Check the pronunciation in your dictionary.

verb	noun	verb	noun
photograph	photographer	advertise	advertisment
indicate	indication	luxury	luxurious
depart	departure	origin	original
economy	economics	obscene	obscenity
operate	operation	fortune	fortunately
		decide	decision

Pronunciation 29

26 Homophones

Many English words have the same pronunciation, but a different spelling and a different meaning. We call these words *homophones*. Here are some examples:

flower /ˈflaʊɚ/ This is a beautiful *flower*.
flour /flaʊɚ/ Mix the *flour* with some milk and sugar.

sweet /swit/ *Sweet* foods are bad for your teeth.
suite /swit/ We stayed in the most expensive *suite* in the hotel.

A Look at these sentences. In each sentence, one of the words in **bold** is wrong for the context. Write the correct words in the crossword below.

Across
3 As soon as the **mail/male** arrives, bring it to my office.
5 We managed to **break/brake** and stop the car before we hit the dog.
7 My father was a sailor, and so was my grandfather. There is a long **navel/naval** tradition in my family.
9 We need some more pens and pencils. Is there a **stationery/stationary** store near here?
11 Are you OK? You look like you're in a complete **days/daze**.
12 Although they live in the ocean, **whales/wails** aren't fish—they're mammals.
13 The **deer/dear** ran across the road right in front of our car.

Down
1 To finish making the dish, **great/grate** some cheese and put it on top of the potato.
2 Five dollars for a hot dog? What a **waste/waist** of money!
4 I'm sorry, but dogs aren't **aloud/allowed** in here.
6 One of the window **pains/panes** has been broken.
8 I hope our business succeeds; there's a lot of money at **steak/stake**.
9 Be careful where you're walking; don't step on my blue **suede/swayed** shoes.
10 The meeting was a **real/reel** disaster.

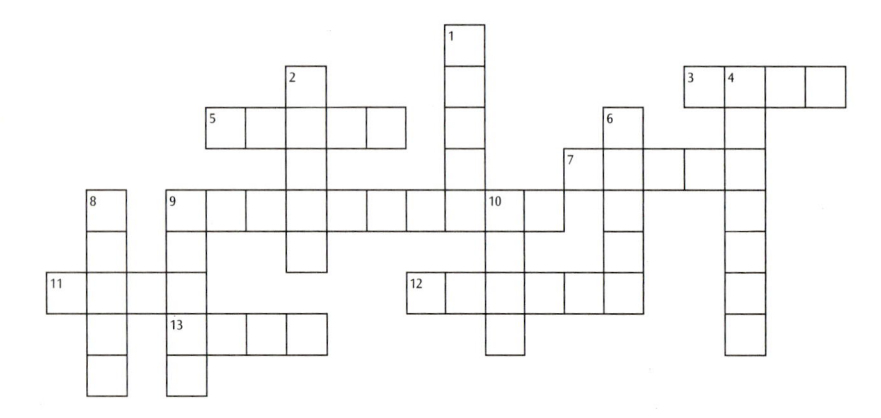

30   Pronunciation

■ **B   Use your dictionary to find other examples of English homophones. Most (but not all) homophones have one syllable, for example, *rain/reign*, *meet/meat*, etc.**

27 Phonetics 1

■ **Draw lines to match the pronunciation symbols in the box with the bold letters in the sentence below it. Each pronunciation symbol should be used only once. There are five symbols in each box that you do not need.**

| θ | eɪ | ɚ | ɑr | dʒ | k | aʊ | tʃ | ɪ | ɑ | æ | ð |

The **qu**i**ck** br**ow**n **f**o**x j**um**p**ed **o**v**er** the l**a**z**y** d**o**g.

| ʊ | ɔr | u | s | ɪ | z | aɪ | ʃ | dʒ | i | tʃ | eɪ |

She sell**s ch**eap b**oo**ks b**y** the **s**ea**sh**or**e**.

| u | i | ɛ | θ | ʌ | aʊ | oʊ | ɚ | aɪ | ð | ŋ | eɪ |

Y**ou** don't kn**ow** a**ny th**ing about m**e** and m**y** b**u**ddies.

Pronunciation   31

28 Phonetics 2

A Look at this information sheet from an international language school. The words in **bold** have a letter or letters underlined. At the end of each word, you will see two pronunciation symbols. One of them shows you the sound of the underlined letter(s), and one of them does not.

Circle the correct pronunciation symbol for each word.

Boston Institute for World Languages
Rules for International Living

It can **some**t**imes** (eɪ, (aɪ)) be difficult **l**i**ving** (i, ɪ) and studying in a foreign country. However, follow **these** (θ, ð) rules, and your stay in Boston will be more pleasant and **enj**o**yable** (ɪ, oʊ) for you, and for those around you.

1 **Am**e**ricans** (ɛ, ə) are always saying **pl**ea**se** (ɪ, i) and **th**ank (θ, ð) you. These are probably the most important words in our **l**a**nguage** (æ, ɑ)! Use them whenever you can.

2 Students at BIWL **c**o**me** (oʊ, ʌ) from all over the world. You **sh**ou**ld** (ə, ʌ) be sensitive to those around you: remember that not everyone **comes** (z, s) from the same **cul**t**ural** (ə, ʊ) background as you. Don't **h**ur**t** (ɪr, ɚ) others' feelings. And don't **j**u**dge** (dʒ, y) others by your own standards.

3 You should speak English at all times, especially if you are in a mixed-nationality **gr**ou**p** (u, ʊ). After all, that is the reason you are **h**ere (ɛr, ɪr)!

4 BIWL is in a residential area. Respect our **n**eigh**bors** (aɪ, eɪ) by keeping noise to a minimum, **espe**ci**ally** (tʃ, ʃ) at night.

5 Be **aw**are (ɛr, ɑr) of those **ar**ou**nd** (oʊ, aʊ) you. For example, don't block the sidewalk so that other people have to walk in the road!

6 Try to help people if they have **pr**o**blems** (ɑ, æ). For example, the next time you see your teacher coming into class with an **arm**ful (ɑr, ɔr) of books, be nice and hold the **d**oo**r** (ɔr, ʊr) open for him or her.

7 Don't **thr**ow (oʊ, aʊ) trash (**ch**ewing (dʒ, tʃ) gum, Coke **bo**tt**les** (t̬, t), etc.) on the ground. Try to keep our college tidy.

8 Don't complain all the time. Remember that nobody or **noth**ing (n, ŋ) is perfect!

9 Make the most of your **lei**s**ure** (ʃ, ʒ) time: come on one of our college **t**ours (ʊr, ɔr), join the college football or baseball teams, or just go for a **w**al**k** (ɑ, ɔ) in our beautiful city.

B Now check the pronunciation of these words in the dictionary.

32 Pronunciation

Collocations

LONGMAN Dictionary of American English

> **sit·u·a·tion** /ˌsɪtʃuˈeɪʃən/ *n.* [C] a combination of all the things that are happening and all the conditions that exist at a particular time and place: *the present **economic/political situation** in the country* | *In this **situation**, it is unrealistic to expect a quick solution.*
>
> **COLLOCATIONS**
> **difficult/bad/dangerous/tough situation** – one that is bad and difficult to deal with
> **economic/political/financial situation**
> **present/current situation** – one that exists now
> **no-win situation** – one that will end badly no matter what you decide to do
> **win-win situation** – one that will end well for everyone involved in it
> If a **situation improves**, it becomes better.
> If a **situation worsens** or **deteriorates**, it becomes worse.

Words that are commonly used with other words are called *collocations*. Common collocations are in **bold** in the example sentences in the dictionary entries. Important words also have Collocation boxes that show typical collocations. For example, look at the entry for *situation*.

29 Example Sentences

> **un·u·su·al** /ʌnˈyuʒuəl, -ʒəl/ *adj.* different from what is usual or normal: *Our team has an unusual number of talented players.* | *unusual clothes* | *It's **unusual for** Dave to be late.*

Example sentences help you understand what a word or expression means, and how to use it. When you use your dictionary, look at the words in **bold** in the sentences and learn which words are used together.

■ Look at the words and their meanings in column A. Correct the mistake in each sentence in column B. Check your answers in your dictionary.

A		B
1	**prefer** to like someone or something more than someone or something else	*I prefer spend my vacation in Hawaii.*
2	**rely** to trust or depend on someone or something	*He's relying with us to get the job done on time.*
3	**lean** to support yourself or be supported in a position that is not straight or upright	*The old man was leaning up a fence.*
4	**proud** feeling pleased because you think that something you have achieved or are connected with is very good	*She's extremely proud with her daughter.*
5	**apply** to make a formal, especially written, request for a job, place at a college, permission to do something, etc.	*She's decided to apply for a college in California.*

Collocations 33

6	arrive to get to a place	*The train arrives at Chicago at about four o'clock.*
7	excited happy, interested, or hopeful because something good has happened or will happen	*Are you excited for going to the baseball game?*
8	object to say that you do not like or approve of something.	*We strongly object the government's proposal.*
9	responsible in charge of or taking care of something	*The airline is responsible to the safety of passengers.*
10	annoyed slightly angry	*The boss was getting annoyed him.*

30 Do, Make, or Take

■ Complete the sentences using a form of the verbs *do*, *make*, or *take*. Check your answers in your dictionary.

How to improve your English

So you want to ___make___ **progress** in classes at school? Well, _____ yourself a **favor** and _____ my **advice**.

First of all, _____ an **effort** to attend all your classes, and _____ your **best** to be on time every day. Try to _____ a **seat** near the front of the classroom; don't hide in the back!

_____ the best **use** of your school's facilities. If your school has a library or a computer room, get in there and use the resources whenever you can.

When you _____ your **homework**, try to _____ your **time**—don't try to finish it too quickly. _____ some **notes** before you start writing. _____ a good **look** at your work afterward to check that you haven't _____ too many **mistakes**.

_____ the **most** of every opportunity to learn. For example, it's a good idea to _____ **friends** with other students so you can study together.

34 Collocations

If you have to _____ a **test** at the end of the class, _____ **sure** that you arrive at school or at the place where the test is going to _____ **place** in plenty of time (_____ a **taxi**, if necessary).

If you can do all this, I'm sure you will _____ **well** in your studies.

31 Collocations 1

■ Some of the words and expressions in the boxes *collocate* with the words in **bold**. Complete the sentences using words from the box. You will not use all the words. Check the Collocation boxes in your dictionary for the words in **bold** for help.

1 You can say that somebody has *leathery* , _____, _____, or _____ **skin**.

| leathery dark silky |
| happy oily sensitive |
| smelly skinny |

2 You can _____, _____, or _____, a **check**.

| ask for split save |
| work out go for pick up |
| poke come across |

3 A **fire** can _____, _____, _____, or _____.

| slow take up rage |
| die down break out |
| talk smolder show up |

4 You can _____, _____, _____, _____, or _____ **interest**.

| show arouse attract |
| express interfere lack |
| experience like |

5 You can _____, _____, _____, _____, _____ an **invitation**.

| affect send out receive |
| take accept |
| turn down go for get |

6 You can _____, _____, _____, or _____ **lunch**.

| bake have go out for |
| nibble peel break for |
| eat cut up |

7 You can speak of a _____, _____, _____, _____, or _____ **marriage**.

| failed mortal pleased |
| long-lived broken |
| troubled loveless happy |

8 You can talk about _____, _____, _____, _____, or _____ **food**.

| overgrown foolish |
| stale frozen nutritious |
| fresh same organic |

Collocations 35

32 Collocations 2

A In each of these sentences, one of the words in *italics* cannot be used with the word in **bold**. Circle that word.

1 **Hair** can be: *shoulder length, frizzy, slim, red, curly*.

2 You can *shake, nod, scratch, clench, turn* your **head**.

3 You can receive *sick, overtime, vacation, health, take-home* **pay**.

4 **Clothes** can be *formal, unofficial, fashionable, loose, dressy*.

5 A store can *increase, raise, cut, lower, demolish* the **price** of its products.

6 You can sit in a(n) *front row, passenger, vacancy, window, aisle* **seat**.

7 People talk about *smooth, difficult, tough, economic, financial* **situations**.

8 You can **sleep** *well, badly, lightly, lately, like a baby*.

9 You can *read, send, reply to, forward, backward* an **e-mail**.

10 You can *give, say, state, express, voice* an **opinion**.

B Check your answers in the Collocation boxes for the words in **bold** in your dictionary.

Grammar

LONGMAN Dictionary of American English

33 Irregular Verbs

Your *Longman Dictionary of American English* shows the *past tense*, *past participle*, and *present participle* forms of all irregular verbs.

> **go¹** /goʊ/ v. past tense **went** /wɛnt/ past participle **gone** /gɔn, gɑn/ third person singular **goes**

There is also a useful list of irregular verbs at the back of your dictionary.
Your dictionary also shows you if a regular verb needs an extra letter before the -ed/-ing ending (for example, *rig, rigged, rigging*).

Additionally, your dictionary shows you the third person singular form of verbs that need an extra letter or letters before the -s ending. (for example, *go, go**e**s*).

■ Complete the table with the correct past tense and past participle forms of the verbs on the left. Be careful—some verbs can have more than one past tense or past participle form! Then check your answers in your dictionary.

	PAST TENSE			PAST PARTICIPLE		
Infinitive	Stays the same	Adds -ed	Has another ending	Stays the same	Adds -ed	Has another ending
become			*became*	*become*		
bite						
burn						
dream						
eat						
grow						
pay						
put						
shake						
shut						
throw						

34 Transitive and Intransitive Verbs

> A transitive verb is a verb that must be directly followed by a noun or object pronoun. (I *love* **you**.)
> An intransitive verb is not directly followed by an object. (She *arrived* at seven-thirty.)
> Some verbs can be transitive or intransitive depending on their meaning, or how they are used. Your dictionary uses the labels [T] or [I] to show you if a verb is transitive, intransitive, or both.
>
> **love**¹ /lʌv/ v. [T] **1** to care very much about someone, especially a member of your family or a close friend: *It's incredible how much she loves those two kids.*
>
> **dream²** v. past tense and past participle **dreamed** or **dreamt** /drɛmt/ **1** [I,T] to have a dream while you are asleep: *I often dream that I'm falling.*
>
> **ar·rive** /əˈraɪv/ v. [I] **1** to get to a place: *Your letter arrived last week.* | *What time does the plane arrive in New York?* | *We arrived at Mom's...*

A Look at these verbs, and decide if they are transitive, intransitive, or both. Write [T], [I], or [I,T]. Check your answers in your dictionary.

pay _____[I,T]_____   wear _____   disappear _____

forget _____   perform _____   contact _____

stay _____   remember _____   wait _____

sleep _____   park _____   carry _____

B Match the first part of each sentence on the left with one or two of the second parts on the right.

1	I can't afford to pay … __e, p__	a… your friend's name
2	Do you think I should wear … _____	b… my car here?
3	He disappeared … _____	c… for you for half an hour, then left.
4	Did you forget … _____	d… and was never heard from again.
5	The group performed … _____	e… you right now.
6	I've been trying to contact … _____	f… that suitcase for me?
7	He stayed … _____	g… with all that noise?
8	I don't remember … _____	h… in his apartment even though it was very dirty.
9	We waited … _____	i… him for the last two weeks.
10	How can you sleep … _____	j… about the party?
11	Can I park … _____	k… so don't keep asking me what happened.
12	Can you carry … _____	l… terribly, and most of the audience left.
		m… songs from their latest album.
		n… in the lot across the road?
		o… this to my interview?
		p… that much for a pair of jeans.
		q… John's address?

38   Grammar

35 Grammar in Use

> **GRAMMAR**
> Use **all** with a singular verb when you are using a U noun: *All the wine is gone.*
> Use **all** with a plural verb when you are using a plural noun form: *All my friends are coming to the party.*
> → EVERY

Grammar boxes in your dictionary explain important grammar rules, and show you how to avoid some common mistakes. For example, look at the word *all*.

A Fill in the blanks with the correct word or words. If you need help, look up the two **bold** words in your dictionary. The Grammar box will be found at one of them.

1	There are _____ cheap apartments to rent than there used to be	**fewer/less**
2	It takes about _____ hour to drive from here to the coast.	**a/an**
3	Unfortunately, **all** the **bread** _____ stale.	**is/are**
4	I'm thinking of buying _____ **same** kind of DVD player as you.	**a/the**
5	There's still _____ ice **tea** left if you'd like it.	**little/a little**
6	He told the police that he hadn't seen _____ acting suspiciously.	**anyone/someone**
7	Chris is _____ superb tennis player.	**so/such** a
8	We'll **try** to **arrive** _____ school just before nine o'clock.	**at/in**
9	**None** of the **food** _____ particularly tasty.	**was/were**
10	There were very _____ people waiting at the bus stop.	**little/few**

B Look at these pairs of sentences. In each case, one is correct, and one is incorrect. Circle the correct one. If you need help, look at the Grammar box for the word in bold in the first column.

1	**enough**	There isn't room enough in the closet.	(There isn't enough room in the closet.)
2	**always**	He goes always fishing on the weekends.	He always goes fishing on the weekends.
3	**the**	The plane arrives at Jacksonville International Airport at six a.m.	The plane arrives at the Jacksonville International Airport at six a.m.
4	**both**	My both brothers play basketball.	My brothers both play basketball.
5	**also**	James can play the piano, and he can also play the flute.	James can play the piano, and he can play also the flute.
6	**far**	It's far to the beach from our hotel.	It's a long way to the beach from our hotel.
7	**the**	It can get very cold at night.	It can get very cold at the night.
8	**never**	She is never in a good mood.	She never is in a good mood.
9	**most**	He likes most of sports, but he really hates swimming.	He likes most sports, but he really hates swimming.
10	**any**	Have you ever eaten a snail?	Have you ever eaten any snail?

Grammar **39**

36 Common Mistakes

Your dictionary can help you to avoid some common mistakes. These are shown in the entry by ▶ ◀.

> **great·ly** /ˈgreɪtli/ *adv. formal* extremely or very much: *The money you lent us was greatly appreciated.* ▶ Don't say "The money was appreciated greatly." ◀

■ Look at these pairs of sentences. In each case, one is correct, and the other one is incorrect. Put an ✗ next to the incorrect one.
Then check your answers in your dictionary. (You will need to decide which word to look up in your dictionary in order to find the answer.)

1	I agree with you.	I am agree with you. ✗
2	He tried to avoid to make mistakes.	He tried to avoid making mistakes.
3	He drives very bad.	He drives very badly.
4	There are a lot of high trees in this park.	There are a lot of tall trees in this park.
5	Sara said she was innocent, but no one believed in her.	Sara said she was innocent, but no one believed her.
6	It will take between six and eight months to complete the work.	It will take between six to eight months to complete the work.
7	I'm bored. Let's go out this evening.	I'm boring. Let's go out this evening.
8	That dress she bought cost very much.	That dress she bought cost a lot.
9	It is common for actors to be anxious before going on stage.	It is common that actors to be anxious before going on stage.
10	Ted has a good job working for a computer company.	Ted has a good work working for a computer company.
11	He's one of the highest people in our class.	He's one of the tallest people in our class.
12	The bus arrived and she got on it.	The bus arrived and she got in it.
13	I wonder what color does her new shoes have.	I wonder what color her new shoes are.
14	You could try contacting him by email.	You could try contacting him with email.
15	I explained him the procedures.	I explained the procedures to him.

40 Grammar

Vocabulary and Wordbuilding

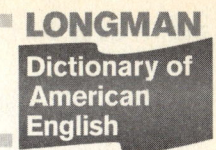

LONGMAN Dictionary of American English

37 Compound Words

A lot of English words are made up of two or more words put together (for example, *sunburn* = *sun* + *burn*), or used together to create a new word or idea (for example, *country music*, *couch potato*, etc.). We call these *compound words*.

Compound words can be found in their own separate entries in your dictionary.

> **ice¹** /aɪs/ *n.* **1** [U] water that has frozen into a solid: *Do you want some ice in your drink?* | *There's too much ice and snow on the roads.* **2 break the ice** to begin to be friendly to someone by talking to him/her: *Stan tried to break the ice by asking her where she was from.*

> **ice·break·er** /ˈaɪsˌbreɪkɚ/ *n.* [C] **1** something you say or do to make someone less nervous **2** a ship that can sail through ice

> **ˌice-ˈcold** *adj.* extremely cold: *ice-cold drinks*

> **ˈice cream** *n.* [U] a frozen sweet food made of milk or cream and sugar, usually with fruit, nuts, chocolate, etc. added to it: *vanilla ice cream*

■ Look at the words in the columns. Match the words on the left to the words on the right, to create compound words: for example *post* and *office*. Then write the compound word on the line. Remember that some need to have a hyphen, some are one word, and some are two words.

post	bag	_____
food	tennis	_____
police	dryer	_____
sleeping	knife	_____
half	lot	_____
sun	time	_____
hair	lights	_____
pocket	board	_____
fast	office	*post office*
income	paste	_____
table	food	_____
ironing	tax	_____
parking	station	_____
tooth	glasses	_____
traffic	poisoning	_____

Vocabulary and Wordbuilding   41

38 Verb Prefixes

A prefix is a short group of letters added to the begining of some words. A prefix changes the meaning of a word, often creating an opposite meaning, for example *agree/disagree*. Your dictionary shows opposite words created by adding a prefix.

> **a·gree** /əˈgri/ v. 1 [I,T] to have the same opinion as someone else [≠ **disagree**]: *I agree with Karen. It's much too expensive.* ▶ Don't say "I

A Look at the verbs in the box and make new words using the prefixes *un-*, *dis-*, or *mis-*.

| agree | appear | approve | behave | connect | continue | fold | like |
| load | obey | place | pronounce | qualify | understand | use | |

B Use the verbs with their prefixes to complete the sentences and fill in the crossword. (You will need to change the form of some of the words, for example, by making them past tense.)

[Crossword grid with 1 Across filled in as DISAGREED]

Across

1 We talked for hours, but _____ about the best way to solve the problem.

6 Five bus routes will be _____ from next week.

7 You've _____ my name; it's Smits, not Smith.

8 You should always _____ electrical equipment before repairing it.

42 Vocabulary and Wordbuilding

9   I've _____ my purse. Have you seen it?

11 Several athletes were _____ from the race because they had cheated.

13 She took the newspaper from her bag and _____ it.

14 The rabbit _____ inside the magician's hat.

Down

2   Her parents were really angry when she _____ their orders and stayed out late.

3   Many people thought the chairman had _____ his power.

4   George has been _____ at school.

5   You must have _____ her. She would never have said that.

8   A lot of people _____ housework.

10 We _____ the boxes from the back of the truck.

12 Her family strongly _____ of her behavior.

39 Adjective Prefixes

Many adjectives can also be made into opposites by adding a *prefix*.

A Work in pairs. Add a prefix (*dis-*, *il-*, *im-*, *in-*, *ir-*, or *un-*) to each adjective to form a new adjective with an opposite meaning. Then check your answers in your dictionary. The student with the most correct answers is the winner.

Student 1 dis- il- im- in- ir- un-	Student 2 dis- il- im- in- ir- un-
___obedient ___regular ___patient	___literate ___honest
___legal ___believable ___accurate	___competent ___mature
___mortal ___attractive	___satisfied ___responsible
___complete ___resistible	___correct ___fair ___fashionable
___agreeable ___logical	___legible ___possible ___rational

B Now write sentences on another sheet of paper, using the adjectives with their prefixes.

C Can you think of any other adjectives that can be made into opposites by adding a prefix?

40 Thesaurus 1: Build your Vocabulary

Thesaurus boxes explain related words that might be used in a different way depending on the context. They also show you how these words work with other words. Thesaurus boxes are a great way of developing your vocabulary.

> **val·u·a·ble** /ˈvælyəbəl, -yuəbəl/ *adj.* **1** worth a lot of money: *a valuable ring*
>
> **THESAURUS**
> **precious** – valuable because of being rare or expensive: *precious gems*
> **priceless** – so valuable that you cannot calculate a financial value: *a priceless painting by Rembrandt*
> **worth a lot/a fortune** – to be worth a very large amount of money: *Their house is now worth a fortune.*

In this box, for example, we can see that *priceless* is often used to describe a *painting*.

■ The words and expressions in boxes A and B are synonyms of the words in *italics* in sentences 1–14. In each case, the synonym has a stronger meaning than the word in the sentence. Match the synonyms with their appropriate sentences. Use the Thesaurus boxes in your dictionary to help you.

Box A
worn out   disgusting   loaded delighted   gripping   petrified sweltering   destitute   deafening furious   ~~outstanding~~   abysmal a rip off   gorgeous

Box B
stunning   electric   ecstatic   boiling atrocious   livid   terrified   rolling in it exhausted   impoverished astronomical   ~~exceptional~~   thunderous revolting

1   He's a *good* football player.   A = <u>outstanding</u>   B = <u>exceptional</u>
2   The applause at the end of the show was *loud*.   A = _____   B = _____
3   Twenty dollars for a pizza? That's *expensive*.   A = _____   B = _____
4   I was *angry* when they canceled the flight.   A = _____   B = _____
5   I always feel *tired* at the end of a semester.   A = _____   B = _____
6   Many Americans were *poor* during the Depression.   A = _____   B = _____
7   I was *happy* when he asked me to marry him.   A = _____   B = _____
8   Your grades are *bad*.   A = _____   B = _____
9   Yuck! This hot dog is *horrible*.   A = _____   B = _____
10 I think my new girlfriend is *attractive*.   A = _____   B = _____
11 My dog is *frightened* when it hears loud noises.   A = _____   B = _____
12 People who are *rich* can be very selfish.   A = _____   B = _____
13 It was *hot* in the classroom.   A = _____   B = _____
14 The atmosphere during the ball game was *exciting*.   A = _____   B = _____

Vocabulary and Wordbuilding

41 Thesaurus 2: Use the Correct Word

■ The word in **bold** in each of these sentences has been used incorrectly. The words at the end of each sentence will guide you to the Thesaurus box in your dictionary where you will find a more appropriate word or words for the sentence. Write the word in the blank.

1   She sat in front of the television **rubbing** the cat. (touch) ___*stroking*___

2   Ugh, this bread is so **rotten** I almost broke a tooth on it. (old) _____

3   His new book is a real **blockbuster**; over 2 million copies have been sold. (popular) _____

4   Water had **spurted** slowly through a small hole in the pipe, and was all over the kitchen floor. (pour) _____

5   Despite **rehearsing** for weeks, the swimmers did very badly in the competition. (practice) _____

6   He **advised** that I see the latest *Harry Potter* movie, because he thought I'd really enjoy it. (advise) _____

7   Jane recently had twins, so she is now on maternity **holiday**. (vacation) _____

8   It took us over half an hour to **stroll** through the deep snow to Bob's place. (walk) _____

9   I'm **underprivileged** until I get paid next week. (poor) _____

10 I feel absolutely **revolting** this morning; I think I'm getting a cold. (horrible) _____

42 Confusing Words

Usage boxes in your dictionary show you words that are often used incorrectly, and the correct way to use them. For example, look at the Usage box for *north*:

> **USAGE**
> Use **north/south etc. of sth** in order to describe where a place is in relation to another place: *Chicago is south of Milwaukee.*
> Use **in the north/south etc. of sth** in order to say which part of a place you are talking about: *The mountains are in the west of the province.*
> Use **northern, southern,** etc. with the name of a place: *They have a cabin in northern Ontario.* Don't say "in the north of Ontario."

■ Work in pairs. The sentences in each box contain two words in **bold**. Only *one* of them is correct. Take turns circling the correct word in each sentence. Then check your answers by looking in the Usage boxes in your dictionary. The winner is the student who chose the most correct words.

Student A

1 Could you **remember/remind** me to go to the post office later?
2 If you have a question, please **raise/rise** your hand.
3 Could you **borrow/lend** me $10? I'll pay you back tomorrow.
4 How much money do you **earn/win** in your new job?
5 The medicine had a really strange **affect/effect** on me.
6 He's a wonderful person, and **fun/funny** to spend time with.
7 You should ask your teacher to **learn/teach** you some basic grammar rules.
8 She's quite **sensitive/sensible**, so please try not to upset her.

Student B

1 I can't lend you the money you need because I don't have **some/any**.
2 Could you **say/tell** me what time the next bus arrives?
3 The movie we saw last night was **really/very** wonderful.
4 I've **lost/missed** my keys. Did I leave them on my desk?
5 OK everyone, I think we're **all ready/already** to leave. Let's go.
6 A gang of men **stole/robbed** the First National Bank last night.
7 She's **too/very** hardworking and intelligent, so I'm sure she'll pass all her classes.
8 She spent most of the day **watching/seeing** television and eating cold pizza.

43 Abstract Nouns

■ Work in pairs. Change the words in bold to nouns. The first student to correctly change all the words into nouns is the winner. Write the nouns in the blanks. Then check your answers in your dictionary.

Student A

1 I think your (**behave**) has been absolutely terrible. _____

2 They looked at me in (**astonish**) when I walked through the door. _____

3 Scientists have made an incredible (**discover**) that could change the world. _____

46 Vocabulary and Wordbuilding

4 He was very handsome in his (**young**). _____

5 My roommate and I had a terrible (**argue**) last night. _____

6 The (**organize**) doesn't have enough money to continue. _____

7 Professor Jenkins doesn't have much (**patient**) for lazy students. _____

8 People say that (**laugh**) is the best medicine. _____

Student B

1 A bank account full of money isn't always a sign of (**succeed**). _____

2 I'm afraid I can't give you (**permit**) to leave early today. _____

3 I don't think I have enough (**confident**) to be an actor. _____

4 We can get you a ticket if there is a (**cancel**). _____

5 Her face went bright red with (**embarrass**). _____

6 It's been a real (**please**) meeting with you. _____

7 If you want to make a (**complain**), I suggest you talk to the manager. _____

8 Do you think that (**happy**) is more important than success? _____

44 Adjective Opposites

As we have seen, many entries in the dictionary show other words that are related (synonyms, opposites, etc.). Learning these related words can increase your vocabulary.

> **mi·nor**¹ /ˈmaɪnɚ/ *adj.* small and not very important or serious, especially when compared with other things [≠ **major**]: *minor surgery* | *We made a few **minor** changes to the plan.* | *It's only a **minor** injury.* ▶ Don't say "minor than." ◀

In this entry, we can see that *major* has the opposite meaning of *minor*.

■ Look at the **bold** words in these sentences, and write their opposites in the blanks. Use your dictionary to help you.

1 The court found her **guilty** of fraud. _____

2 There's a **deep** pool in our yard. _____

3 His doctor told him that there was some **permanent** damage to his muscles. _____

4 Houses in this area used to be very **cheap**. _____

5 Some foods have **artificial** colors added to them. _____

6 The point on this pencil is really **sharp**. _____

7 He's a good **amateur** golfer. _____

8 This cream is supposed to keep your skin **smooth**. _____

9 This loaf is **stale**. _____

10 Carry this bag—it's fairly **light**. _____

45 Topic Vocabulary

> **TOPIC**
> When you get into a car, you **buckle/fasten your seatbelt**, then put the key in the **ignition** and turn it to **start the engine**.
> You **release** the **parking/emergency brake**, and put the car in **drive**. You **check your mirrors** (=look into them) before driving onto the street. You press the **gas pedal** with your foot to make the car **accelerate** (=go faster).
> When you turn right or left, you must **indicate/put on your turn signals**. When you want to slow down, you press the **brake (pedal)** with your foot.
> When you **park** your car, you put the car **in park** and **set/put on the parking brake**.

In your dictionary you will find lots of Topic boxes, which contain words and expressions used to talk or write about a particular topic or theme. For example, look at the word *drive*:

■ Work in pairs. Take turns looking at the sentences in your table. Write where the speakers are, using the words in bold to help you. Choose from the different places in the box below. Check your answers at the Topic boxes for *theater*, *office*, etc. in your dictionary. Give yourself 1 point for each place you correctly identified. The winner is the student with the most points.

a theater   an office   an airport   a bank   a wedding   a restaurant   a hotel

	Student A	The speaker is at/in:
1	Doesn't the **bride** look beautiful?	
2	We need to be at the **gate** in 15 minutes.	
3	How much are the **programs**?	
4	The service was terrible. I'm not leaving a **tip**.	
5	Everybody here has their own **workstation**.	
6	You can **check in** as soon as the other guests have left.	
7	Could you give me my **balance**?	
8	Are you sure that this is the correct **terminal**?	
9	I'd like to **withdraw** everything, please.	
10	The **reception** begins immediately after the service.	

	Student B	The speaker is at/in:
1	There's nothing on the **menu** that I really like.	
2	I'd like to **deposit** this check, please.	
3	The coffee machine is over there by the **file cabinets**.	
4	The **groom** looks really nervous, doesn't he?	
5	We've got a great seat up in the **balcony**.	
6	It can take ages to get through **security** this time of day.	
7	Do you have **room service** here?	
8	Hi, I'm Mike. I'm the **best man**.	
9	There will now be a half-hour **intermission**.	
10	I don't really want an **appetizer**.	

48   Vocabulary and Wordbuilding

46 Computers and the Internet

A Circle the word from each pair in **bold** that correctly completes the text. Check your answers in the Topic boxes at *computer* and *Internet*.

I've been teaching my parents how to use their computer. I showed them how to plug it in, how to (1) **fire/boot** it up, and how to (2) **log on/sign up**.

At first, my parents said they just wanted to type (3) **documents/papers** using word processing software. My mother always forgot how to (4) **unfold/open** a (5) **software/file** when she wanted to start working on it, and my father never remembered to (6) **save/record** his work so he could continue working on it later. Gradually, they became more confident and even learned how to (7) **readjust/reboot** their computer after it (8) **crashed/broke down**.

Then they asked me to show them how to use the Internet. I helped them (9) **sign up/connect** to it using a (10) **modem/cell phone** that sends information through telephone wires into their computer. This type of connection is very slow. If you have a (11) **broadband/super** connection, it is much faster. My parents had the (12) **zip codes/addresses** of specific (13) **networks/websites** they wanted to visit. I showed them how to search the whole Internet using a (14) **search engine/searchlight**. Soon, they had been spending so much time (15) **scanning/surfing** the web that they knew exactly what to do. They showed me the (16) **newsgroups/news offices** (= sites where people with a shared interest exchange messages) and (17) **chat rooms/talk centers** (= sites where you can have a conversation with other people) that they visit. Now whenever they have a question they send it to me by (18) **e-messages/e-mail**!

47 The Environment

Unscramble the letters in **bold**. The first letter of each answer has been underlined. Write the words in the grid. A secret word connected with the environment will appear in the shaded column. Check your answers in the Topic box for *environment* and elsewhere in your dictionary.

1 Rain that contains acid chemicals from factory smoke and cars, etc. (**cdai inra**)
2 A word describing material that can be destroyed by natural processes, in a way that does not harm the environment. (**igobdebaraled**)
3 An area of thick forest with tall trees that are very close together, growing in a place where it rains a lot. (**inarsofrte**)
4 The warming of the air around the Earth as a result of the sun's heat being trapped by pollution. (**resehoguen fcfete**)
5 A compound word describing products that are not harmful to the environment (**ceo-rideynfl**)
6 To put materials such as paper and glass through a special process so that they can be used again. (**yececrl**)
7 The protection of natural things such as animals, plants, forests, etc. (**eronstcionva**)
8 To spoil something by adding a dangerous or poisonous substance to it. (**amontiacten**)
9 An increase in world temperatures, caused by pollution in the air. (**blogla ainwgrm**)
10 Damage caused to air, water, soil, etc., by harmful chemicals and waste. (**oltipuonl**)
11 A word used to describe food or farming that does not use chemicals that are harmful to the environment. (**gniorca**)
12 Someone who is concerned about protecting the environment. (**iresnanvonemtlit**)
13 A word describing a type of plant or animal that soon might not exist anymore (an _____ species). (**anegdneerd**)

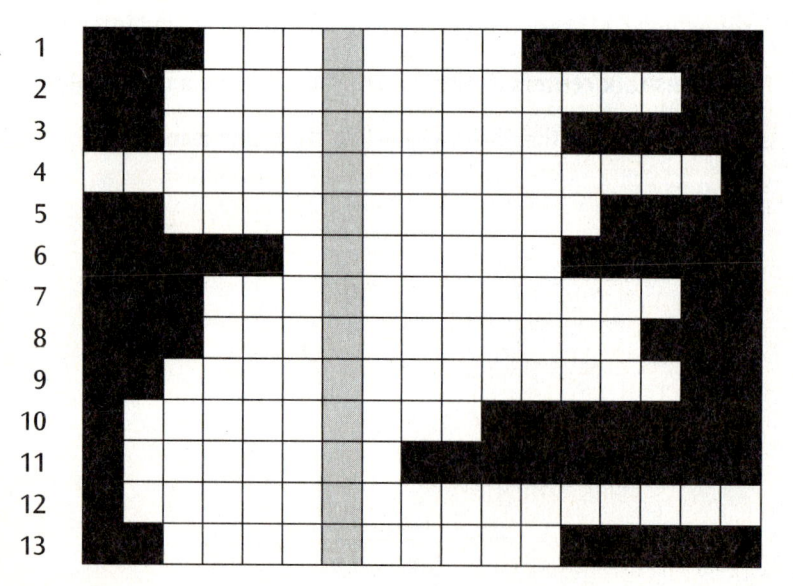

50 Vocabulary and Wordbuilding

48 College

Complete the text using the words from the box. Use the Topic box at *university* to help you.

minor	classes	subject	graduates	midterm
seminars	laboratory	general education	professors	graduate
final	lectures	college	teaching assistants	quarter
major	papers	students	semester	degree
credits				

Brad goes to (1) _____ in Boston. His (2) _____ (= main subject to study) is physics and his (3) _____ (= second (4) _____ to study) is French. He also studies music, chemistry and geography so that he has a good (5) _____. He is one of the most hard-working (6) _____ in college and always gets good grades in the (7) _____ exams and in the (8) _____ exams which take place at the end of each (9) _____ or (10) _____ (= periods of time that the college year is divided into). He seldom misses any of the (11) _____, (12) _____, or (13) _____ taught by the (14) _____ and (15) _____ (= (16) _____ students in the subject they are teaching). He has to write (17) _____ and do (18) _____ work in order to earn enough (19) _____ for each class. When he (20) _____, he hopes that his (21) _____ will help him to find a good job.

Vocabulary and Wordbuilding 51

49 Travel

A Read this description of air travel. Unscramble the letters in bold and complete the crossword. The first letter of each word or expression has been underlined.

Two weeks ago I had to go to Mexico on a business trip. My **glihft** (17 across) was at 10 a.m. so I had to get to the **etramlin** (12 down) about two hours before then. First of all, I had to **hkcce ni** (15 across) (= show my ticket, leave my bags, etc) at the check-in **nocurte** (11 across) and then I had to go through airport **urecsyit** (13 down) where they check all the passengers and their bags to see if they are carrying anything dangerous like a knife or a gun. After that, I had to wait in the **trpdeareu gloeun** (14 across) for quite a while. Eventually my flight **menurb** (3 down) was called and I went through the boarding **geta** (9 down) before **ribgoadn** (2 across) (= getting on the plane). I always get very nervous just before the airplane **steak fof** (6 down) from the **wnayru** (16 across) and always feel much happier when the plane **sladn** (5 across) at the end of the journey. Fortunately it was a smooth flight this time. After I got off the plane, I went through **migimionrat** (8 across) where I had to show my **tossprpa** (1 down). Next, I found my way to the **geagbga** (7 across) **mlaic** (4 down) where I got my suitcase back. Before leaving the airport I went through **scumsto** (10 across) where my bags were checked.

B Look at the Topic box for *airport* in your dictionary to check your answers.

50 Jobs

A Complete the text using the correct words from the box. Don't forget to put the words in the correct form. Some of the words are not used.

résumé	fire	heading	Help Wanted	salary	hand in
retire	job listings	apply for	pull	notice	promote
promotion	invite	application form	reference	fill	increase
interview	offer	finish	cover letter		

When she graduated from college, Kirsty decided to get a full-time job, so she started looking at the (1) _job listings_ section in the newspapers. She also checked out the (2) _____ signs in store windows. She eventually found a job that sounded good, and decided to (3) _____ it. She (4) _____ out an (5) _____ and sent it off, together with her (6) _____ and a (7) _____ introducing herself. The company she wanted to work for asked for a (8) _____, so Kirsty gave them the name of her math professor, with whom she had always gotten along.

A few days later, she was (9) _____ to an (10) _____, and was really happy when she was (11) _____ the job. She did well in the company, and after a few months she got (12) _____. As part of this (13) _____, she was given an (14) _____ in her (15) _____.

Unfortunately, a couple of years later, a new manager took over her department. He and Kirsty didn't get along very well, and Kirsty threatened to (16) _____ her (17) _____ unless the manager was replaced. Luckily, the manager got (18) _____ before Kirsty had to quit. Kirsty is still working for the company, and hopes to do so until she (19) _____ when she's 65.

B Check your answers in your dictionary at the Topic box for *job*.

Phrasal Verbs

LONGMAN Dictionary of American English

51 Phrasal Verb Chain

Phrasal verbs can be found at the end of the entries for the verbs that are used to create them. For example, look at the word *press*:

> **press on/ahead** *phr. v.* to continue doing something without stopping: *The army crossed the river and pressed on to the border.*

■ Complete the sentences with the phrasal verbs in the box. The last letter of each phrasal verb that you use is the *first* letter of the next phrasal verb you will use. You will have to change the form of some of the phrasal verbs.

bring up	fall through	find out	hand in	hold off
put off	pull through	run across	set up	take over

1. After her husband died, she had to ___bring up___ the children on her own. (*to educate and care for a child until s/he is old enough to be independent*)

2. The boss is likely to _____ tomorrow's meeting until next week. (*to delay something, or to delay doing something*)

3. The police are trying to _____ who robbed our house. (*to learn information after trying to discover it, or by chance*)

4. When their father retires, the two brothers will _____ the company. (*to take control of something*)

5. She _____ some old photographs while cleaning out the attic. (*to meet or find someone or something by chance*)

6. They want to _____ their own import-export business. (*to start a company, organization, business, etc.*)

7. After the accident, the doctors were not sure if he would _____. (*informal: to stay alive after a serious injury or illness*)

8. Buyers are _____ until the price falls. (*to delay doing something*)

9. The deal _____ because the two sides couldn't agree on a price. (*to fail to happen or be completed*)

10. Don't forget to _____ your homework before you leave. (*to give something to someone in a position of authority*)

52 Hidden Phrasal Verbs

A Find the 12 phrasal verbs hidden horizontally and vertically in the word search below.

| point out | pick up | break out | put off | put up with | come in |
| fall for | make up | make out | own up | get together | look up to |

A	B	F	A	L	L	F	O	R	C	G
D	M	A	K	E	U	P	E	F	G	E
H	P	I	J	K	L	I	M	N	O	T
P	U	Q	R	S	T	C	U	P	V	T
W	T	B	R	E	A	K	O	U	T	O
M	O	L	O	O	K	U	P	T	O	G
A	F	M	Z	A	B	P	C	U	D	E
K	F	A	F	O	W	N	U	P	T	T
E	H	K	I	J	K	L	M	W	N	H
O	P	E	Q	C	O	M	E	I	N	E
U	P	O	I	N	T	O	U	T	S	R
T	U	U	V	W	X	Y	Z	H	A	B

B Now replace the word in **bold** with the correct phrasal verb from part A. Change the form if necessary. Use your dictionary to help you. These phrasal verbs can all be found in the Thesaurus boxes after the words in **bold**.

1 Prison security is being improved to stop the prisoners from **escaping**. _breaking out_

2 I refuse to **tolerate** your behavior any longer. _____

3 I'm just going to the store to **buy** some milk. _____

4 He thought the plan would work, but I **said** that there would be some problems. _____

5 She finally **admitted** to breaking my camera. _____

6 I really **admire** people who work hard in order to succeed. _____

7 I'll meet you at the airport when your flight **arrives**. _____

8 Why don't we **meet** this weekend? _____

9 The radio said all men over 50 would have to take a driving test every year, and I **believed** it! _____

10 In the distance we could just **see** a faint light. _____

11 We decided to **delay** the meeting until the following week. _____

12 My grandfather used to **invent** stories to tell us when we were children. _____

Phrasal Verbs 55

53 Phrasal Verb Combinations

A Work in pairs. Combine the words in Box B with the verbs in Box A to make phrasal verbs, for example, *carry off*, *carry on*, etc. Give yourself one point for each correct combination. Who scored the most points?

Box A: Verbs

carry come cut fall get give go look make pick put run set take turn

Box B: Prepositions and Adverbs

about	across	after	along	around	at	away	back
behind	by	down	for	forward	in	into	off
on	out	over	through	to	up		

carry off, carry on, carry out, carry over, carry through

_____

_____

_____

_____

_____

_____

_____

B Now choose six phrasal verbs that you found and write your own sentences.

1 _____

2 _____

3 _____

4 _____

5 _____

6 _____

Idioms

LONGMAN Dictionary of American English

54 True or False Idioms

Idioms and other informal and/or spoken expressions can usually be found in the entry for the first noun in the idiom or expression. If the idiom appears at a different word, an arrow will show you where to look.

goat /goʊt/ *n.* [C] **1** a common farm animal with horns and with long hair under its chin → see picture at FARM¹ **2 get sb's goat** *informal* to make someone very angry or annoyed

brain¹ /breɪn/ *n.* **1** [C,U] the organ inside your head that controls how you think, feel, and move: *brain damage* | *the part of the brain that controls movement* → see picture on page A3 **2** [C usually plural, U] the ability to think clearly and learn quickly: *The kid's definitely got brains.* **3** [C] *informal* someone who is very intelligent: *Some of the best brains in the country are here tonight.* **4 be the brains behind sth** to be the person who thought of and developed a particular plan, system, organization, etc. → NO-BRAINER → **pick sb's brain(s)** at PICK¹ → **rack your brain(s)** at RACK²

■ Look at these sentences, and decide if they are True or False. Check your answers in your dictionary.

1. If someone says, "*Make yourself at home*," they want you to come and visit them. ☐ True ☐ False

2. A *slave driver* is someone who makes people work very hard. ☐ True ☐ False

3. A *couch potato* is someone who enjoys cooking. ☐ True ☐ False

4. Someone who is *doing time* is in the hospital. ☐ True ☐ False

5. People who *play with fire* often take risks or do dangerous things. ☐ True ☐ False

6. A good student always *plays hooky*. ☐ True ☐ False

7. If you are *under the weather*, you are angry because it is raining. ☐ True ☐ False

8. If you have just *paid through the nose* for something, you didn't spend much money on it. ☐ True ☐ False

9. When you go *the whole hog*, you do something thoroughly and completely. ☐ True ☐ False

10. People who are *on cloud nine* are dead. ☐ True ☐ False

11. Something that is described as being *out of this world* is very good. ☐ True ☐ False

12. People who *make a killing* have to go to prison. ☐ True ☐ False

55 Body Part Idioms

These idiomatic expressions can all be completed using a part of the body. Complete each one with an appropriate word. Use the pictures to help you.

You will find each idiom in your dictionary under the entries for the different parts of the body.

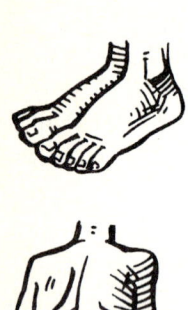

1. Come in, sit down, put your _____ up and relax.

2. I told him not to do it, but he went behind my _____ and did it anyway.

3. I can't come out tonight. I'm up to my _____ in work.

4. He has his _____ full right now, so he's probably too busy to help you.

5. My boss likes to make us work hard. He always keeps us on our _____.

6. Don't embarrass him. He hates to lose _____ in front of others.

7. We will fight _____ and nail to make sure the school stays open.

8. I earn so little money that it's really difficult to keep my _____ above water.

9. You worked so hard—you should come out with us tonight and let your _____ down.

10. Good luck on your test tomorrow. I'm keeping my _____ crossed for you.

11. We don't see _____ to _____. We disagree about everything.

12. She thinks she's perfect, and looks down her _____ at everyone else.

13. This room is too small for all of us. Let's go outside where we can have some _____ room.

14. Ed's wife has him under her _____. He does everything she says.

15. When we found out the company was going to reduce our salaries, we were all up in _____.

58 Idioms

56 Idiom Groups

■ **Complete the sentences to make idioms. Check your answers in your dictionary.**

Idioms with Colors

Choose from these colors:
black   green   gray   blue   red

1 We almost never see her. She only visits us *once in a* _____ *moon*.

2 What are the laws about downloading things from the Internet? It seems like a _____ *area* to me.

3 If I'm not *in the* _____ at the end of this month, I won't be able to pay my bills.

4 He's usually very calm, but he *saw* _____ when I broke his camera.

5 Your plants are beautiful. You really *have a* _____ *thumb*.

Idioms with Animals

Choose from these animals:
bird   bull   pig   rat   cat

1 Ronnie's party was supposed to be a surprise. Who *let the* _____ *out of the bag*?

2 He got sick of *the* _____ *race* and quit his job.

3 It's a difficult problem, but if we *take the* _____ *by the horns*, we'll solve it.

4 Whenever Bob and Steve order pizza, they really _____ *out on* it.

5 She's a real *early* _____, and always gets to work before seven o'clock.

Idioms with Food

Choose from these foods:
cake   milk   bananas   meat   peanuts

1 The test wasn't difficult. In fact, it was a *piece of* _____.

2 I work *for* _____ and never have enough money to go out on Fridays.

3 She *went* _____ when I told her that I had found another girlfriend.

4 If he hasn't returned my CDs by tomorrow, he's *dead* _____!

5 He's a very wealthy man, so I'm planning to _____ him for every cent he's got!

Idioms with Clothes

Choose from these clothes:
shoes   hat   sleeve   socks   boot

1 This movie is fantastic. It will *blow your* _____ *off*!

2 *I wouldn't like to be in your* _____ when Dad finds out you broke the window.

3 Our boss has a few surprises *up his* _____, and will tell us more at the meeting.

4 She's wealthy, attractive, and has a good sense of humor *to* _____.

5 He has a few secrets that he's keeping *under his* _____.

Idioms   59

Communication

57 Spoken Phrases

> **SPOKEN PHRASES**
> **4 this/that kind of money** a phrase meaning a lot of money, used when you think something costs too much, when someone earns a lot more than other people, etc.: *The rent was $5,250, and I just don't have that kind of money.* **5 pay good money for sth** to spend a lot of money on something: *I paid good money for those shoes!* **6 for my money** used when giving your opinion about something, to emphasize that you believe it strongly: *For my money, Williams was a much*

Your dictionary has Spoken Phrases boxes, which contain common spoken phrases using certain key words. For example, look at the word *money*:

■ Look at this very informal conversation between two old friends. Fill in the blanks. Look at the Spoken Phrases in your dictionary for the words in **bold** to help you.

Andy: _____ there, Todd. **How**'s it _____? Everything OK?

Todd: I **guess** _____, Andy. But I'm having a few problems at work.

Andy: _____ **come**? _____ the **matter**?

Todd: It's my new boss. He's a real jerk, **let** me _____ you!

Andy: Oh, I know _____ how you **feel**. But **life**'s too _____ to worry about things like that, you know.

Todd: Sure, but **believe** _____ not, I've never met anyone who's so bad at his job. **Come** to _____ of it, I could do the job better than him.

Andy: I don't like my boss either. He is always in a bad mood. _____ his **problem**, but I don't think he's ever said anything nice to me.

Todd: It really **blows** my _____ that these people get to be in charge.

Andy: Well, I've got to **get** _____. I have to go to a meeting, and I'm already **cutting** it _____. **Tell** you _____, give me a call and we'll get together next week.

Todd: OK, it's been good seeing you, Andy. **Catch** you _____.

Andy: Sure thing, Todd. And you **hang** in _____, buddy.

58 Spoken Expressions

> **COMMUNICATION**
> **Ways of accepting**
> **yes, please**: *"Would you like some wine?" "Yes, please."*
> **I'd love to**: *"Why don't you come over for dinner?" "Thanks, I'd love to."*
> **that sounds nice/good/great/(like) fun**: *"Let's go see a movie." "That sounds great."*
> **sure** spoken: *"Do you want to come with us?" "Sure."*
> **why not?** informal spoken: *"Try one of these*
>
> Communication boxes in your dictionary show you different expressions that we can use in different situations.
>
> See also the Communication Guide in your dictionary on pages A59–A74.

■ **A** Work in pairs. You will need three coins. *Two* of them should be different (for example, a dime and a quarter). Place the two different coins in the "Start" box on the game board below. These will be your playing pieces. Take turns using the third coin like dice. Flip the coin and catch it. If it lands *heads* up, move your playing piece *two* places. If it lands *tails* up, move your playing piece *one* place.

Look at the situation in each box that you land on, and use your dictionary to find out what you should say in that situation. You will find the correct expressions in the Communication boxes at the entries for the words in bold. The first student to reach the "Finish" box is the winner.

Start ▷	A friend of yours has a bad cough and would like some **advice**. ▷	Someone has offered you a ride home, but you've got your own car. **Refuse** the ride. ▷	You have just lost your friend's cell phone. **Apologize** to her. ◁
Introduce one of your friends to another of your friends. ◁	◁ You are going to the theater, but you are worried you might be late. Tell your friend to **hurry**.	◁ You are meeting some very important people for the first time. Say **hello** to them.	◁ Go back to Start
Your friend is having dinner at your house. **Offer** her something to drink. ▷	Go forward 2 spaces	Ask your teacher for **permission** to leave class early. ▷	Some students in your school library are making too much noise. Ask them to be **quiet**. ◁
Somebody asks you what you think of your school. Give her your **opinion**. ◁	Go back 3 spaces	◁ You work in a store and have just helped a customer. Say **goodbye** to him.	◁ Your teacher says something, but you don't understand her. Ask her to **repeat** what she said.
A friend asks if you want to go to see a movie. **Accept** the invitation. ▷	Somebody says that math class is hard. **Agree** with him. ▷	Go back 2 spaces	Finish

■ **B** Now play the game again, this time *without* using your dictionary. Try to remember the different expressions that you should use.

Answers

1 Word Order
painter = 1 painting = 2 palace = 3
palatial = 4 perish = 5 perishable = 6
Ph.D. = 7 phonetic = 8 plaster of Paris = 9
play-by-play = 10 phrase = 11 poised = 12
poisonous = 13 pollution = 14
polyester = 15 psalm = 16 psychology = 17

2 Using Guidewords
area code armchair arable arithmetic
arduous Arctic

3 Labels
A 1 adjective 2 uncountable 3 literary
4 trademark 5 informal 6 singular
7 nonstandard 8 approving 9 something
10 technical 11 phrasal verb 12 preposition

B The word in the shaded column is *intransitive*.

4 Key Words
A There are 5 active words on page 3: about[3], above, absence, absolute, absolutely.
B 1 always 2 keep 3 record 4 new 5 word
6 expression 7 that 8 you 9 learn

5 Cross-Referencing
A 1 housework 2 roof 3 choice 4 laptop
5 bull 6 a saucer 7 depth 8 heroine 9 pony
10 pans/jug 11 an inpatient 12 No, a tree is *tall*.
B stepfather health food early bird
seat belt human being floppy disk
index finger love affair right angle
blackboard financial aid party animal

6 Dictionary Orientation Quiz
1 c 2 b 3 At the phrase *aid and abet* at the entry for *aid*. *Abet* is usually only used as part of this expression. 4 *Abide* is usually used only with the word *can't*. 5 c 6 b 7 approximately. 8 b 9 c 10a *completely totally entirely utterly*. 10b See the Thesaurus box at *completely*. 11 At the entry for *painting*, where you will see a picture. 12 In the Topic box at *drive*, where you will see the word used in a short piece of text. 13 The Communication box at *accept* gives five ways of accepting: *yes, please; I'd love to; sure; why not?* 14 acclimatize. 15 *get your act together, get in on the act.* 16 No. The Usage box contains information comparing these two words. 17 b

7 Definition Quiz 1
1 (normally) a writer 2 just before Easter (late winter/early spring) 3 b 4 your dentist
5 false—they are old. 6 a 7 deer 8 silk
9 a king or queen 10 money 11 d 12 a fish

8 Definition Quiz 2
1 b
2 a dime = 10 cents, a quarter = 25 cents, a nickel = 5 cents
3 quarters
4 b
5 false. It is called The Star-Spangled *Banner*.
6 g
7 The House of Representatives
8 District of Columbia
9 b
10 elementary
11 d
12 watch a movie
13 dance
14 The belief that everyone in the U.S. has the opportunity to be successful if he or she works hard.

9 Picture This
Across: 3 eggplant 5 thumb 7 scarf
9 portrait 10 eyelash 11 hop 12 bench
13 grate
Down: 1 slipper 2 blanket 4 mustache
6 bracelet 7 seed 8 flashlight 12 bagel

10 Which Meaning?
1 meaning 2   4 meaning 3   7 meaning 1
  meaning 1   meaning 5   meaning 2
2 meaning 3   5 meaning 3   8 meaning 8
  meaning 1   meaning 1   meaning 3
3 meaning 1   6 meaning 1
  meaning 3   meaning 4

11 Parts of Speech
Part of Speech
1 adjective
2 noun
3 verb
4 verb
5 preposition
6 noun
7 adverb
8 verb

12 Two Meanings
1 climate = 5, 9
2 depressed = 2, 7
3 medicine = 1, 6
4 generous = 4, 10
5 study = 3, 8

13 Signpost Matching
A
move: She turned and *ran* away.
be in charge of sth: Beth *runs* a bar in Soho.
in a race: I've decided to *run* in the Boston Marathon.
machines: Some cars *run* on diesel.
computers: Check that the software will *run* on your computer.
election: He is *running* for a seat in the Senate.
money/numbers: Inflation was *running* at 10.5%.
news/stories/advertisements: We decided to *run* an ad in the *Houston Chronicle*.
water/liquids: Tears started to *run* down her cheeks.
B
one idea: He made several useful *points* at yesterday's meeting.
main idea: I wish you'd get to the *point*!
purpose: The whole *point* of this new law is to protect people.
in time/development: At that *point* in my life I was still single.
quality: One of his weak *points* is that he easily gets upset.
game/sport: The Los Angeles Lakers are leading by four *points*.
small spot: The stars shone like *points* of light in the sky.
in numbers: Two *point* four million dollars were spent on the project.
place: I waited for her at the *point* where the two paths meet.
C
telephone: I told him I'd *call* him sometime later today.
describe: She *called* him an idiot for wasting his money.
ask/order: You'd better *call* the police.
arrange: I decided to *call* the meeting for Friday afternoon.
say/shout: "Wait for me!" Bob *called*.
name: What are you going to *call* the new puppy?
read names: We had to go stand in line when he *called* our names.

14 Fun with Puns
1 bright 2 change 3 atmosphere
4 charge 5 bar 6 horns 7 beat 8 call
9 bill 10 cracked

15 Consonants and Consonant Groups
watch: ki**tch**en, na**t**ure, pi**c**ture, **ch**eck
key: come, **qu**ick, **c**ream, **k**ind
fantastic: **ph**ysical, lau**gh**, **f**orget, **f**ruit
settle: psychology, **c**oncert, **sc**ene, **s**ee
ship: ma**ch**ine, **s**ugar, **sh**ore, **s**tation
night: knee, **n**ever, **kn**ow, **pn**eumonia
right: wrong, **rh**ino, **h**urry, **r**ice
gaze: result, **z**ebra, day**s**, ari**s**e
jump: judge, **j**acket, **j**aguar, e**dg**e
pen: poetry, **p**eace, o**p**en, **p**ay
heavy: per**h**aps, **h**igh, **h**ello, **wh**o
Wednesday: water, **wh**at, for**w**ard, **wh**en
game: guest, a**g**ree, fin**g**er, **g**opher
thing: theater, **th**ink, **th**eory, pa**th**
the: ga**th**er, **th**ere, **th**ough, **th**at

16 Vowels and Vowel Groups
B
pull and *rough* do not contain the same sounds as the other words in the group.
C
beat:	feed suite achieve ceiling
bit:	typical
date:	paid weigh gauge break campaign
bat:	laugh
bet:	threat said
book:	would
box:	father
but:	mother touch
bought:	dog wall caught jaw
boat:	tone throw
banana:	photograph fasten wonderful generality
shirt:	murder
bite:	style buy eye height
about:	how
voice:	boy
beer:	dear weird
bare:	stair bear
door:	bored more roar

17 Plurals
1 knifes→knives 2 abilitys→abilities
3 potatos→potatoes 4 pianoes→pianos
5 countrys→countries 6 womans→women
7 mediums→media 8 busses→buses
9 persons→people (*persons* is sometimes used in more formal situations)
10 mouses→mice

18 More Than One Spelling
1 enroll 2 dialogue 3 pricey 4 gray
5 glamour 6 Jell-O 7 disk 8 catalog

19 Common Spelling Mistakes
Across
4 persistent 7 government 10 achieve
11 benefited 13 coal 5 style 16 contain
17 advertising 18 argument 21 overweight
22 gnarled 26 knowledge 27 photographs
28 peaceful 29 separate
Down
1 gauge 2 pronunciation 3 attic
5 fluency 6 absences 8 efficient
9 challenging 10 advised 12 campaign
14 canceling 15 science 19 typical
20 wrinkles 23 drought 24 touch
25 beard

20 Identifying Pronunciation
A bomb *and* shock **B** watchful

21 Syllables 1
1 ex•pro•pri•ate 2 fra•grance 3 op•er•ate
4 o•rig•i•nal 5 sym•pa•thet•ic
6 in•di•ca•tion 7 doubt 8 de•funct
9 seis•mic 10 realm 11 lux•u•ri•ous
12 in•cin•er•ate 13 Wednes•day
14 re•tire 15 warped 16 pi•geon
17 in•volve•ment 18 ad•ver•tise•ment
19 dis•cus•sion 20 phy•sique 21 hair•style

22 Syllables 2
1 Syllable cracked hedge cooked laugh
2 Syllables crooked compute junior fruitless
3 Syllables radio fruition classified sympathize
4 Syllables advertisement enjoyable indication overburdened
5 Syllables justifiable representative unfortunately periodical

23 Stressed Syllables
A
• shows syllable breaks. The stressed syllables are in **bold**.
a•**bout** sea•son•al a•**gree**•a•ble
em•**ploy** ac•**com**•pa•ny **ar**•ro•gant
pho•**tog**•ra•pher **hock**•ey se•**cu**•ri•ty
pro•**nounce** ap•**pear**•ance **se**•ri•ous•ly
ad•jec•tive con•**clu**•sion **teach**•er
ar•gu•ment
B
• shows syllable breaks. The main stress is in **bold**. The secondary stress is underlined.
ac•a•**dem**•ic ac•<u>com</u>•mo•**da**•tion
<u>af</u>•ter•**shave** <u>al</u>•pha•**bet** ar•ti•**fi**•cial
as•<u>sas</u>•si•**na**•tion

24 Stress Change 1
A The stressed syllables of the nouns are underlined: <u>in</u>crease, <u>in</u>sult, <u>con</u>duct, <u>re</u>fund, <u>pre</u>sent, <u>ob</u>ject, <u>re</u>bel, <u>per</u>mit, <u>des</u>ert, <u>pro</u>duce (or pro<u>duce</u>), <u>sus</u>pect, <u>pro</u>test
B
1	protest	6	produce
2	refund	7	insult
3	permit	8	increase
4	rebel	9	object
5	present	10	desert

25 Stress Change 2
The stressed syllables are shown in bold.

pho**tog**rapher, indi**ca**tion, de**par**ture, eco**nom**ics, ope**ra**tion, adver**tise**ment, lu**xu**rious, o**rig**inal, ob**scen**ity, **for**tunately, de**ci**sion

26 Homophones
A
Across: 3 mail 5 brake 7 naval
9 stationery 11 daze 12 whales 13 deer
Down: 1 grate 2 waste 4 allowed
6 panes 8 stake 9 suede 10 real
B
There are many homophones in the dictionary. Compare with friends or ask your teacher to look at your list.

27 Phonetics 1
Th(ð)e q(k)uick brow(aʊ)n fo(ɑ)x j(dʒ)umped over(ɚ) the la(eɪ)zy dog.
Sh(ʃ)e sells(z) ch(tʃ)eap boo(ʊ)ks by(aɪ) the sea(i)shore(ɔr).
You don't know(oʊ) a(ɛ)nyth(θ)ing(ŋ) about me(i) and my(aɪ) bu(ʌ)ddies.

28 Phonetics 2
It can **sometimes** (aɪ) be difficult **living** (ɪ) and studying in a foreign country. However, follow **these** (ð) rules, and your stay in Boston will be more pleasant and **enjoyable** (ɔɪ) for you, and for those around you.

1 **Americans** (ɛ), *please* (i), **thank** (θ), **language** (æ)
2 **come** (ʌ), **should** (ə), **comes** (z), **cultural** (ə), **hurt** (ɚ), **judge** (dʒ)
3 **group** (u), **here** (ɪr)
4 **neighbors** (eɪ), **especially** (ʃ)
5 Be **aware** (ɛr), **around** (aʊ)
6 **problems** (ɑ), **armful** (ɑr), **door** (ɔr)
7 **throw** (oʊ), **chewing** (tʃ), **bottles** (t)
8 **nothing** (ŋ)
9 **leisure** (ʒ), **tours** (ʊr), **walk** (ɔ)

29 Example Sentences
A
1 prefer **to** spend my vacation in Hawaii.
2 He's relying **on** us to get the job done on time.
3 The old man was leaning **against** a fence.
4 She's extremely proud **of** her daughter.
5 She's decided to apply **to** a college in California.
6 The train arrives **in** Chicago at about four o'clock.
7 Are you excited **about** going to the baseball game?
8 We strongly object **to** the government's proposal.
9 The airline is responsible **for** the safety of passengers.
10 The boss was getting annoyed **with** him.
B
The example sentences show us how a word or expression works with other words (in this case, all the words are followed by a specific *preposition*. The example sentences show us which preposition(s) can be used.

30 Do, Make, or Take
(although some other verbs are possible in some cases)
So you want to *make* **progress** in school? Well, *do* yourself a **favor** and *take* my **advice**. First of all, *make* an **effort** to attend all your classes, and *do* your **best** to be on time every day. Try to *take* a **seat** near the front of the classroom; don't hide in the back!
Make the best **use** of your school's facilities. If your school has a library or a computer room, get in there and use the resources whenever you can.
When you *do* your **homework**, try to *take* your **time**—don't try to finish it too quickly. *Make* some **notes** before you start writing. *Take* a good **look** at your work afterward to check that you haven't *made* too many **mistakes**.
Make the **most** of every opportunity to learn. For example, it's a good idea to *make* **friends** with other students so you can study together.
If you have to *take* a **test** at the end of the class, *make* **sure** that you arrive at school or

Answers

at the place where the test is going to *take place* in plenty of time (*take a taxi*, if necessary).
If you can do all this, I'm sure you will *do well* in your studies.

31 Collocations 1
1 You can say that somebody has leathery, dark, oily, or sensitive **skin**.
2 You can ask for, split, or pick up a **check**.
3 A **fire** can break out, die down, smolder, or rage.
4 You can show, arouse, attract, express or lack **interest**.
5 You can receive, send out, accept, turn down, or get an **invitation**.
6 You can have, go out for, break for, or eat **lunch**.
7 You can get a telephone, email, text, or fax **message**.
8 You can speak of a failed, happy, broken, troubled, or loveless **marriage**.
9 You can talk about stale, frozen, nutritious, fresh, or organic **food**.

32 Collocations 2
1 slim 2 clench 3 health 4 unofficial
5 demolish 6 vacancy 7 smooth 8 lately
9 backward 10 say

33 Irregular Verbs
PAST TENSE

Infinitive	Stays the same	Adds -ed	Has another ending
become			became
bite			bit
burn		burned	burnt
dream		dreamed	dreamt
eat			ate
grow			grew
pay			paid
put	put		
shake			shook
shut	shut		
throw			threw

PAST PARTICIPLE

Infinitive	Stays the same	Adds -ed	Has another ending
become	become		
bite			bitten
burn		burned	burnt
dream		dreamed	dreamt
eat			eaten
grow			grown
pay			paid
put	put		
shake			shaken
shut	shut		
throw			thrown

34 Transitive and Intransitive Verbs
A
pay [I,T] wear [T] disappear [I] forget [I,T] perform [I,T] contact [T] stay [I] remember [I,T] wait [I] sleep [I] park [I,T]

B
1 e, p
2 o
3 d
4 j, q
5 m, l
6 i
7 h
8 a, k
9 c
10 g
11 b, n
12 f

35 Grammar in Use
The words in parentheses after each answer show where information on the grammar point can be found in the dictionary.
A
1 fewer (less)   6 anyone (someone)
2 an (a)   7 such a (such)
3 is (all)   8 at (arrive)
4 the (same)   9 was (none)
5 a little (little²) 10 few (few)

B
1 There isn't enough room in the closet for all my clothes.
2 He always goes fishing on the weekends.
3 The plane arrives at Jacksonville International Airport at six a.m.
4 My bothers both play basketball.
5 James can play the piano, and he can also play the flute.
6 It's a long way to the beach from our hotel.
7 It can get very cold at night.
8 She is never in a good mood.
9 He likes most sports, but he really hates swimming.
10 Have you ever eaten a snail?

36 Common Mistakes
Correct sentences:
1 I agree with you.
2 He tried to avoid making mistakes.
3 He drives very badly.
4 There are a lot of tall trees in this park.
5 Sara said she was innocent, but no one believed her.
6 It will take between six and eight months to complete the work.
7 I'm bored. Let's go out this evening.
8 That dress she bought cost a lot.
9 It is common for actors to be anxious before going on stage.
10 Ted has a good job working for a computer company.
11 He's one of the tallest people in our class.
12 The bus arrived and she got on it.
13 I wonder what color her new shoes are.
14 You could try contacting him by email.
15 I explained the procedures to him.

37 Compound Words
sleeping bag   table tennis   hairdryer
pocket knife   parking lot   half-time
traffic lights ironing board post office
toothpaste   fast food   income tax
police station sunglasses   food poisoning

38 Verb Prefixes
A
disagree   disappear   disapprove
misbehave disconnect discontinue
unfold   dislike   unload   disobey
misplace/displace (note the different meanings) mispronounce disqualify
misunderstand misuse

B
Across: 1 disagreed 6 discontinued
7 mispronounced 8 disconnect
9 misplaced (not *displaced*) 11 disqualified
13 unfolded 14 disappeared
Down: 2 disobeyed 3 misused
4 misbehaving 5 misunderstood 8 dislike
10 unloaded 12 disapproved

39 Adjective Prefixes
Student 1
disobedient irregular impatient illegal
unbelievable inaccurate immortal
unattractive incomplete irresistible
disagreeable illogical
Student 2
illiterate dishonest incompetent
immature dissatisfied irresponsible
incorrect unfair unfashionable illegible
impossible irrational

40 Thesaurus 1
1 outstanding exceptional   2 deafening thunderous   3 a rip off astronomical
4 furious livid 5 worn out exhausted
6 destitute impoverished 7 delighted ecstatic 8 abysmal atrocious 9 disgusting revolting 10 gorgeous stunning
11 petrified terrified 12 loaded rolling in it 13 sweltering boiling 14 gripping electric

41 Thesaurus 2
1 **stroking**
2 **stale**
3 **bestseller**
4 **dripped/leaked**
5 **training**
6 **recommended**
7 **leave**
8 **trudge**
9 **broke**
10 **terrible/awful**

42 Confusing Words
Student A:
1 remind 2 raise 3 lend 4 earn 5 effect
6 fun 7 teach 8 sensitive
Student B:
1 any 2 tell 3 really 4 lost 5 all ready
6 robbed 7 very 8 watching

43 Abstract Nouns
Student A
1 **behavior**
2 **astonishment**
3 **discovery**
4 **youth**.
5 **argument**
6 **organization**
7 **patience**